WHY DO MEN
STUPEFY THEMSELVES?

Why Do Men Stupefy Themselves?

and other writings by

Leo Tolstoy

Translated by Aylmer Maude

Edited by Meredith Murray
and the Editors of 24 Magazine

STRENGTH BOOKS
A Division of East Ridge Press
Hankins, N.Y. 12741 U.S.A.

Distributed by Steinerbooks, Blauvelt, N.Y. 10913

Library of Congress catalog card number: 74-16880
ISBN: 0-914896-08-3

Pictures

What is the explanation?

Contents

Commentaries by the Editors of 24 Magazine:

COMMENTARY I: Pharmacolatry,
    the Religion of the Present Age   15

COMMENTARY II: The Very Strange Case
    of What Has Happened to Drugs and
    Drugging in the New Testament   23

Leo Tolstoy's Essays:

WHY DO MEN STUPEFY THEMSELVES?   39

THE FIRST STEP   73

INDUSTRY AND IDLENESS   127

And further, by these, my son, be admonished: of making books there is no end: and much study is a weariness of the flesh.

Let us hear the conclusion of the whole matter: Fear God, and keep his commandments: for this is the whole duty of man.

Eccles. 12:12-13

Publisher's Note

We are bookmakers who specialize in the literature of the Way. It needs saying that in the pursuit of the Way, books can be well used or abused. Reading is helpful and in most cases necessary, but it is no substitute for *doing the work* of the Way in obedience to the will of God.

This is a serious matter. Hear what a great master of the spiritual life (Caussade) says:

"The divine influence alone can sanctify us. . . . Without it reading only darkens the mind. . . . All reading not intended for us by God is dangerous. It is by doing the will of God and obeying his holy inspirations that we obtain grace, and this grace works in our hearts, through our reading or any other employment. Apart from God, reading is empty and vain and, being deprived for us of the life-giving power of the action of God, only succeeds in emptying the heart by the very fullness it gives to the mind.

"This divine will, working in the soul of a simple ignorant girl by means of sufferings and actions of a very ordinary nature, produces a state of supernatural life without the mind being filled with self-exalting ideas; whereas the proud man who studies spiritual books merely out of curiosity receives no more than the dead letter into his mind, and, the will of God having no connection with his reading, his heart becomes ever harder and more withered."

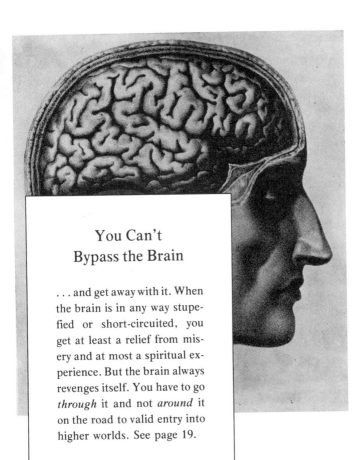

You Can't
Bypass the Brain

. . . and get away with it. When
the brain is in any way stupefied or short-circuited, you
get at least a relief from misery and at most a spiritual experience. But the brain always
revenges itself. You have to go
through it and not *around* it
on the road to valid entry into
higher worlds. See page 19.

Pharmacolatry—the Religion of the Present Age

Almost alone among the men of his time, Leo Tolstoy foresaw the accelerating degenerative trend in the religious life of our race from the worship of God to the worship of mind-altering chemicals. In our day it has reached epidemic and catastrophic proportions.

The one deeply believed-in religion of the present age binds men not to God but to potent, malevolent spirits who will give men what they want—for a time—for a price. This religion may properly be called pharmacolatry, the worship of drugs. The use of drugs for excitement, pleasure, courage, mental and physical ease, psychic power, and ecstatic experience—the practical, seven-day-a-week-religion that finds security, comfort, and joy in chemicals—has swept our culture and put all other religions in the shade. The drugs please their worshippers by performing instantly and efficiently as promised. There is really only one thing wrong with this beautiful picture: in the long run it is a disaster.

You do not have to guess at the extent of drug use in this country; the federal government has taken pains to measure it. Here are the figures for use and abuse of various kinds of drugs by youths and adults of both sexes as given in the Shafer Commission Report in 1973: Regular users of alcoholic beverages: 80,057,420. Regular users of cigarettes: 57,347,970. Non-medical users of proprietary sedatives, tranquilizers, and stimulants: 11,278,480. Non-medical users of prescription sedatives, tranquilizers, and stimulants: 23,456,600. Marijuana users: 29,337,240. Users of LSD and other hallucinogens: 7,625,044. Users of glue and other inhalants: 4,529,174. Cocaine users: 4,546,343. Heroin users: (the smallest of all) a mere 1,966,492.

It is an impressive score for drugs even allowing for the fact that not all users are hooked or addict users, or even necessarily regular users, except in the case of alcohol and cigarettes. But behind the above figures there is still one more statistic that is the most revealing of them all. It concerns the *medical*, or so-called legitimate use of ethical sedatives, tranquilizers, and stimulants. What the Shafer Commission reported was only the *non-medical* use of these substances, that is, self-admitted spree, or pleasure-oriented use by those people surveyed. This is merely the visible part of the iceberg. The truly massive, dedicated dependence on drugs shows up precisely in the medical area. Of all prescriptions written annually, a very high percentage is written for *psychotropics*, mood- and mind-altering chemicals. The aggregate number of prescriptions written at the present time for these drugs is huge; in 1970 the figure was up to 214 million and increasing seven percent a year, which would bring it to

280 million this year. From sixty to seventy percent of the entire adult population are at least occasional medical users of psychoactive drugs.

So that is one side of the picture: millions upon millions of respectable adult men and women going off regularly to doctor and pharmacist for their ration of psychic release and comfort. The other side of the picture was filled in just last September by Dr. Morris E. Chafetz, director of the National Institute of Alcohol Abuse and Alcoholism, who reported among other recently surveyed facts about alcohol, that fourteen percent of senior high school men get drunk at least fifty-two times a year. Chafetz said in a press conference that the statistic "just blows my mind."

And well it might. While there is nothing new in the idea of self-stupefaction through drugs, and men have been doing it as far back as the record goes, what is new is the sheer extent of it. Well over half of our population of 200 million is involved, and not just with old standbys like alcohol and tobacco but with a host of fancy new agencies for stupefaction widely available today. What is all the drugging about? What purpose is served by this very nearly incredible total of chemical tampering with brains and nervous systems?

It is not that people set out to be naughty and wicked, and do things their mothers told them not to. You have to assume that people do all this drugging in search of something they feel is very good. And what is that? They are searching for *connection*. They want to be hooked up, plugged in, on the high wire, alive, aware. In other words, they want the blissful higher consciousness that is traditionally associated with profound development of the spiritual life. Mind-altering drugs are short cuts to that higher consciousness. They lift a dull, dry-as-dust person caught in ordinary twentieth century meaninglessness and everyday routine—for a time—up to a place where the air sings and the best and most intense hopes are about to be realized. All of us desperately want genuine comfort in life, the comfort that comes from knowing that our lives amount to something; we want courage to face what faces us; we want release from overconcern with self. We want to have great friendships, to love and be loved, and in short to live where the face of Nature is brightest and most transcendent. These are the deepest yearnings of mankind, and there is nothing wrong with the yearnings. What is wrong is finding and settling for bogus religion and illegitimate short-cuts, which end by producing the complete reversal of those very good things we yearned for: comfort turns into misery, courage into weakness, friendship and love into hatred, the love of God's creation into sick, narcissistic absorption in one's own moods and feelings.

The kind of comfort for conscience, soul, and body that people seek in drugs is a kind of comfort we are all meant to have. In fact we are designed for very much more than any drug can release, and the word for what we are designed for is no mere middle-class, mediocre commodity like comfort; it is nothing less than joy. Here is a critical term representing an irrefragable reality. Joy—the word itself—has been debased in English. In the New Testament it is *makarios*: bliss, the one irreversible positive emotion which has no opposite, the goal and summit of all possible human emotional and intellectual experience.

There is a way to approach this joy. The New Testament is a highly coded formulary for achieving it. The first command of Christ in his earthly ministry was: *metanoeite*. This word which is usually translated *repent* literally means *go beyond mind*. Surely it is not hard for a modern man or woman who has experienced drugged

states to understand what is pointed to here: it is necessary to get above ordinary modes of thought if we are to
have direct spiritual experience. We certainly never will
have any in our ordinary, self-absorbed, humdrum condition of mind. But many people mistakenly conclude
that the quickest and best way to transcend thought is to
simply go around the brain. That is what the LSD user is
doing, and that is what the drinker is doing when he
blots out his worries by taking a few late-afternoon cock-
tails.

The mind-altering or mood-changing drugs have the
effect of bypassing and to some extent cutting out the
brain. This is true of all of them, including the common-
place and ubiquitous nicotine. Aldous Huxley took some
pains to point out the possibility that the brain acts literally as a reducing valve on reality. If a man were suddenly to take in the whole glory and brilliance of the universe,
it would shatter him as a human being. The brain serves
to cut down the intensity and power of infinite Reality, to
reduce it to manageable and practicable proportions.
What we perceive through the brain's agency is the ordinary three-dimensional world-in-time with all of its interest and charm but at the same time with all of its in-
sufficiencies and frustrations.

When brain function is reduced, we experience some
release from the vexations, the responsibilities, and the
burdens of day-to-day living, and we get a taste of the
untroubled, serene existence that lies above this space-
time manifold. But this release through drugs is bought
at a high price, and the process by which the price is
exacted is an exceedingly interesting one. The great
medieval philosophers and psychologists distinguished
two major functions of the mind—reason (*ratio*) and
intellect (*intellectus*). *Intellectus* is the higher of the two
functions. It is the locus of both intelligence and will

19

(*voluntas*) and the seat of Holy Wisdom; it is the spiritual rudder of our whole being; it is where man is meant to meet and worship God. But reason is the specifically human function; it is the capacity to distinguish relationships (*ratios*) and preeminently the relationship of right to wrong, the ability to compare, classify, judge, measure, and to make simple, plain, garden-variety good sense.

It is reason that is defied and scorned and stunted by drug use, and without reason a man is no man; he descends to the animal and below. Pascal observed that the man who wants to play the angel will end up playing the beast. And the drugger is proof of the maxim. By using drugs to short-cut our way into the realm of *intellectus,* we end up shorn of *ratio,* the ordinary human capacity to defend ourselves against evil and idiocy. The confirmed drugger is wide open to all kinds of error and foolishness, and he loses even the capacity to see that that is his condition.

Leo Tolstoy sensed how big an issue was involved in the modern mass use of mood-changing drugs when he wrote "Why Do Men Stupefy Themselves?" His great statement on drug use in contemporary society is such a landmark because he is practically the only writer of his time—and one of the very few writers ever—who has seen how seriously humanity is threatened by mass drugging. In this area, Tolstoy is literally a prophet for our time.

The simple truth is that drugs are not a way to enlightenment, and they are not a way to real deliverance from psychic suffering. To have any hope of achieving these goals, a human being needs a brain which is in full working order, not one which has been throttled down, hyped up, or tuned out by drugs. We can learn through prayer and meditation to control our thinking and eventually to expand it, contract it, or suspend it, at will. But we cannot short-circuit the mental function mechanically or chemically without opening ourselves up to a take-over by delusions which will abort the whole regenerative process in us.

How well the authors of the New Testament understood that fact is the subject of the second of these commentaries, following.

The statistics in this commentary are taken from *Drug Use in America, Problem in Perspective;* Second Report of the National Commission on Marihuana and Drug Abuse (Washington, D.C., 1973: U.S. Government Printing Office) and from *Licit and Illicit Drugs:* The Consumers Union Report on Narcotics, Stimulants, Depressants, Inhalants, Hallucinogens and Marijuana—including Caffeine, Nicotine and Alcohol (Boston, 1972: Little Brown and Company.)

El Greco: **St. Jerome**

Drugs and Drugging in the New Testament

Tolstoy's intense religious and moral life was bound to Christ's Gospel as a body to its head. But if, as seems likely, the great Russian searched the scriptures for light on the question of men's stupefying themselves with drugs, he could have found not the inkling of an answer. The sacred books appear to be silent on the subject.

What the Bible is really saying sometimes gets twisted and sometimes gets altogether lost in translation. What the Bible says about drugs and drugging is an example— a unique, spectacular, and almost incredible example— of how an urgent and pertinent warning has been fuzzed and finally obliterated in a millennia-old process of juggling the words around. Our civilization's most widely known and deeply respected moral and ethical authority appears to have *nothing at all* to say on the subject of drug abuse. If you look for the word "drug" in any exhaustive concordance of the Bible (for example, Strong's) you will find that it does not occur once either in the Old or New Testament. How has this come about?

Mind-changing, mood-altering, and addictive drugs were used in ancient times. Could it be that Christ and Moses and the prophets did not care if their people got stoned? It is not likely. Or perhaps the problem of drug-taking simply did not exist at that time in anything like the form it does today. Maybe the pressures of modern society have driven men to seek psychic release in drugs—narcotics, psychedelics, amphetamines, barbiturates, tranquilizers, anti-depressants, and mood-elevators—on a scale that the ancients could not have suspected in advance. Again, not likely. How could the prophets and apostles have failed to anticipate the drug problem, since by their office and calling they possessed and repeatedly demonstrated the God-given power to see the shape of things to come?

It makes a tremendous difference whether or not the scripture contains any foresight, any warning, any prophecy on the subject of drug-taking. As a matter of fact it does, in five places, all of them in the New Testament, and four of the five in the Revelation of St. John the Divine, which is a book of prophecy about the times of the end—our times.

What is said about drugs is relevant, powerful, and indispensably instructive. But you or I, unaided, would never be able to dig it out and make sense of it. Not from the most painstaking reading of any of the best-known English translations of the Bible, old and new, Catholic and Protestant. The problem is not obscurity in sentence structure or concept. The meaning of all five passages becomes perfectly clear *once you correct for a misleading translation of one word, essentially the same word, in*

24

each of the passages.

The Greek word is *pharmakeia* (or its close relative *pharmakos*). The original and primary meaning of *pharmakeia* is "drugging". It also has a secondary meaning, "poisoning," and a third meaning, "sorcery." In nearly all the English-language translations of the Bible, from the Tyndale New Testament of 1526 right through the New International Version of 1973, the original and primary meaning of *pharmakeia*—drugging—is totally ignored, and the word is misleadingly given as the last and least significant of its meanings, sorcery (or some synonym of sorcery)*. The only translation from the original Greek which we have been able to find that correctly renders *pharmakeia* is a Greek interlineary version of the New Testament by B.F. Westcott and F.J. Hort, done in 1881 and no longer in print. (For a fuller look at how the various translations have dropped this ball, see the chart on page 33.)

The result of this misreading of *pharmakeia* is that in the critical places where the authors of the New Testament were talking about the use of drugs, our English Bibles have them talking about something else—something that for the modern reader has no connection with drugs. What, after all, is sorcery to 20th century men or women, that they should concern themselves much with it? Sorcery is the "use of power gained from the assistance or control of evil spirits. . . ." (Webster). Most of us, on the rare occasion when we think of sorcery at all, regard it as something considerably less than a major contemporary problem.

---

* The fourteenth century Wycliffe Bible translated this key word as "venemyngis" (poisonings). But the source text for the Wycliffe Bible was the Latin Vulgate rather than the original Greek. Venemyngis is a rendering, not of the Greek *pharmakeia*, but of the Vulgate's Latin *veneficia*.

Here are the New Testament passages containing the word *pharmakeia* and its related forms. The version in the left-hand column is uncorrected—that is, the truncated translations of *pharmakeia* are left in. The version in the right-hand column has been corrected by supplying the original, primary meaning of *pharmakeia*. The rendering of the New Testament presented here is the King James Version, but keep in mind that virtually all of the English language translations of the Bible contain the same mistranslation of *pharmakeia* (see page 33).

UNCORRECTED	CORRECTED
Now the works of the flesh are manifest, which are these, adultery, fornication, uncleanness, lasciviousness, idolatry, witchcraft, hatred, variance, emulations, wrath, strife, seditions, heresies, envyings, murders, drunkenness, revelings, and such like: of the which I tell you before, as I have also told you in time past, that they which do such things shall not inherit the kingdom of God.	Now the works of the flesh are manifest, which are these, adultery, fornication, uncleanness, lasciviousness, idolatry, drugging, hatred, variance, emulations, wrath, strife, seditions, heresies, envyings, murders, drunkenness, revelings, and such like: of the which I tell you before, as I have also told you in time past, that they which do such things shall not inherit the kingdom of God.

Galations 5:19-21 · *Galations 5:19-21*

And the rest of the men which were not killed by these plagues yet repented not of the works of their hands, that they should not worship devils, and idols of gold, and silver, and brass, and stone, and of wood; which neither can see, nor hear, nor walk: neither repented they of their murders, nor of their sorceries, nor of their fornication, nor of their thefts.	And the rest of the men which were not killed by these plagues yet repented not of the works of their hands, that they should not worship devils, and idols of gold, and silver, and brass, and stone, and of wood; which neither can see, nor hear, nor walk: neither repented they of their murders, nor of their druggings, nor of their fornication, nor of their thefts.

Revelation 9:20-21 · *Revelation 9:20-21*

And a mighty angel took up a stone like a great millstone, and cast it into the sea, saying, Thus with violence shall that great city Babylon be thrown down, and shall be found no more at all. And the voice of harpers, and musicians, and of pipers, and trumpeters, shall be heard no more at	And a mighty angel took up a stone like a great millstone, and cast it into the sea, saying, Thus with violence shall that great city Babylon be thrown down, and shall be found no more at all. And the voice of harpers, and musicians, and of pipers, and trumpeters, shall be heard no more at

all in thee; and no craftsman, of whatsoever craft he be, shall be found any more in thee; and the sound of a millstone shall be heard no more at all in thee; and the light of a candle shall shine no more at all in thee; and the voice of the bridegroom and of the bride shall be heard no more at all in thee: for thy merchants were the great men of the earth; for by thy sorceries were all nations deceived.

Revelation 18:21-23

He that overcometh shall inherit all things; and I will be his God, and he shall be my son. But the fearful, and unbelieving, and the abominable, and murderers, and whoremongers, and sorcerers, and idolaters, and all liars, shall have their part in the lake which burneth with fire and brimstone: which is the second death.

Revelation 21:7-8

He that is unjust, let him be unjust still; and he which is filthy, let him be filthy still: and he that is righteous, let him be righteous still: and he that is holy, let him be holy still. And, behold, I come quickly; and my reward is with me, to give every man according as his work shall be. I am Alpha and Omega, the beginning and the end, the first and the last. Blessed are they that do his commandments, that they may have right to the tree of life, and may enter in through the gates into the city. For without are dogs, and sorcerers, and whoremongers, and murderers, and idolaters, and whosoever loveth and maketh a lie.

Revelation 22:11-15

all in thee; and no craftsman, of whatsoever craft he be, shall be found any more in thee; and the sound of a millstone shall be heard no more at all in thee; and the light of a candle shall shine no more at all in thee; and the voice of the bridegroom and of the bride shall be heard no more at all in thee: for thy merchants were the great men of the earth; for by thy drugging were all nations deceived.

Revelation 18:21-23

He that overcometh shall inherit all things; and I will be his God, and he shall be my son. But the fearful, and unbelieving, and the abominable, and murderers, and whoremongers, and druggers, and idolaters, and all liars, shall have their part in the lake which burneth with fire and brimstone: which is the second death.

Revelation 21:7-8

He that is unjust, let him be unjust still; and he which is filthy, let him be filthy still: and he that is righteous, let him be righteous still: and he that is holy, let him be holy still. And, behold, I come quickly; and my reward is with me, to give every man according as his work shall be. I am Alpha and Omega, the beginning and the end, the first and the last. Blessed are they that do his commandments, that they may have right to the tree of life, and may enter in through the gates into the city. For without are dogs, and druggers, and whoremongers, and murderers, and idolaters, and whosoever loveth and maketh a lie.

Revelation 22:11-15

For years I have read and reread the New Testament warnings against sorcery. It never occurred to me that this was something which a highly-civilized, well-brought-up fellow like myself actually needed to be steered away from. I figured in a vague sort of way that sorcery was black magic (whatever that was), and since I was not drawn to bat's wing stews or even to ouija boards, I should just pass on to other areas like anger, lust, and sloth, where I did experience temptation from time to time.

I was shocked awake by an article in the *Cancer News Journal* (1973 volume 8 number 4) by Richardson and Kell entitled "The Biblical Position with Respect to Drugs." The linguistic findings of that article were so striking that a group of the editors of *24 Magazine* researched the matter further until some clarity began to emerge in a remarkably clouded situation.

The primary meaning of *pharmakeia* is familiar enough to us in English from the many words having to do with drugs that are formed from it:

> pharmacy—a drug store
> pharmacist—a druggist
> pharmaceuticals—prepared drugs
> pharmacology—the science of drugs; the properties and reactions of drugs
> pharmocopoeia—an official book listing and describing drugs

For reasons which remain a mystery to us, the Bible translators almost without exception have passed over the original and primary meaning of "drugging" in favor of the tertiary meaning of "sorcery" or "witchcraft". The sense of the verses containing *pharmakeia* is radically altered—and illuminated—when you use the original, literal meaning of the word (see pages 26 and 27 for comparative translations using the uncorrected mistranslations and the corrected translations of *pharmakeia*).

When you read the corrected versions of these passages, you find that Paul classes drugging with adultery, drunkenness, and murder and warns the Galatians that druggers will be cut off from the kingdom of heaven. And the Book of Revelation indicts drugging as a grievous wrong which will become very widespread and be unrepented in the times of the end. The Revelation classes druggers with murderers, thieves, and pimps, and it warns that they are heading for the most serious kind of trouble possible for a human being.

All of this is among the most significant and weightiest prophecy of all time. Obviously the prophecies are coming true in our age, and the warnings are utterly relevant to the current scene. If they were to receive proper circulation they could give life-saving guidance to millions of druggers, including people on the edges of the drug world who may not even know they have a problem—pot-smokers who are attempting to be on a spiritual trip, housewives who convince themselves it is all right to take tranquilizers regularly because "they are not that strong," or moderately upset people who are being maintained on "ups" or "downs" for no reason except that no one knows what else to do for them.

For a large majority of our people the Bible is still a deeply revered guide for living. That is why it remains the best-selling book in the world. Communication of the Biblical warnings against drug-taking would effectively influence more people—young and old—than any other possible kind of public information activity.

The Bible speaks with authority, especially in a case where it is addressing an ill which it correctly foresaw almost 2,000 years ago. And most drug users, especially in the early, pre-hooked stages, are apt to be receptive to any presentation on the subject which comes from people who know what they are talking about, as Paul and John obviously did.

But back to the question of how modern, English-speaking society got cut off from an understanding of the scriptural injunctions against drugging—how *pharmakeia*, in the course of successive translations of the New Testament, came to be stripped of its original and true meaning.

Of the many translations of the original Greek New Testament into English, the most popular and influential has been the King James Version, which was completed in 1611. The traditional title page states that it was "translated out of the original tongues and *with the former translations diligently compared and revised*" [our italics]. The translators were not working solely with the Greek text but also drew upon earlier translations.

One of the chief among these was the Vulgate, a translation from the Greek into Latin finished by St. Jerome in 404. The Vulgate was the first translation of the whole Bible and it may be the most important one ever done. It was the only Bible known in the West during the Middle Ages and has continued to be highly venerated right up to the present. It was still regarded as the official Bible of the Roman Catholic church when the New Catholic Encyclopedia was published in 1967. Needless to say, the Vulgate carried great weight with the committee of scholars who produced the King James Version.

Pharmakeia in the original Greek New Testament was rendered as *veneficia* in the Latin Vulgate, and then as "sorcery" in the English King James Version. A look at the definitions of these three words indicates an interesting pattern: *Pharmakeia* has three meanings;

30

veneficia retains only two of these; "sorcery" retains only one of the original three, and that in a less specific sense than either the Latin or Greek. So the successive translations did not produce equivalents but words progressively weaker in meaning content than the original.

Pharmakeia means drugging, poisoning, or sorcery. *Veneficia* loses the specific, root reference to drugging—a crucial loss. But it still retains a close relationship with the drugging concept by implication. The two meanings of *veneficium* are (1) a poisoning, and (2) the preparation of magical draughts, magic, sorcery. Clearly, the preparation both of poison and of magical draughts involves the use of drugs. And it seems equally clear that neither *pharmakeia* nor *veneficium* ever referred to sorcery-in-general, but that both words referred specifically to drug-sorcery.

Relating back to the Webster definition of sorcery as "the use of power gained from the assistance or control of evil spirits," both *pharmakeia* and *veneficium* apply specifically to a drug-related use of power coming from evil spirits.

Granting that *veneficium* is a weaker word than *pharmakeia* in that it does not say "drugging" with the same force, the drug connotation is strong enough that fifth century Christians reading the Vulgate would have picked it up and made no mistake about it.

But with the translation of *pharmakeia* or *veneficia* into English as sorcery—not drug-sorcery, but sorcery-in-general, any old kind of sorcery—a change of a different order took place. There are numerous forms of sorcery besides drug-sorcery: incantation-sorcery, fetish-sorcery, sorcery-by-touch, and sorcery-by-gaze, to name a few. When you take a word whose root means drug and which itself originally meant drugging, poisoning,

31

Here is how some of the best-known English-language translations of the Bible render the words *pharmakeia* and *pharmakos*, which appear a total of five times in the New Testament. *Pharmakeia* is translated in every case as sorcery, or its synonyms: witchcraft, magic arts, magic, magic spells, practice of magic, practice of spiritism. *Pharmakos* is translated in every case as sorcerer, or its synonyms: fortune-teller, one who practices magic arts, one who practices magic, one who practices spiritism. In no case is there any suggestion of drugs or drugging. The original, primary meaning has been completely lost in every one of these translations.

	pharmakeia original meaning: (1) drugger (2) poisoner (3) sorcerer			**pharmakos** original meaning: (1) drugging (2) poisoning (3) sorcery	
	GALATIANS 5:20	REVELATION 9:21	REVELATION 18:23	REVELATION 21:8	REVELATION 22:15
King James Version	witchcraft	sorceries	sorceries	sorcerers	sorcerers
Douay Version	witchcrafts	sorceries	enchantments	sorcerers	sorcerers
Revised Standard Version	sorcery	sorceries	sorcery	sorcerers	sorcerers
The New English Bible	sorcery	sorcery	sorcery	sorcerers	sorcerers
The Jerusalem Bible	sorcery	witchcraft	spell	fortune-tellers	fortune-tellers
Confraternity New Testament	witchcrafts	sorceries	sorcery	sorcerers	sorcerers
The New American Bible	sorcery	sorcery	sorcery	sorcerers	sorcerers
The New International Version	witchcraft	magic arts	magic spell	those who practice magic arts	those who practice magic arts
Knox Translation	witchcraft	sorceries	sorceries	sorcerers	sorcerers
Moffatt Translation	magic	magic spells	magic spells	sorcerers	sorcerers
Goodspeed Translation	sorcery	magic arts	magic	those who practice magic	those who practice magic
Phillips Translation	witchcraft	sorceries	witchery	traffickers in sorcery	sorcerers
New World Translation	practice of spiritism	spiritistic practices	spiritistic practice	those practicing spiritism	those who practice spiritism
The Amplified New Testament	sorcery	practise of magic (sorceries)	magic spells and poisonous charm	practisers of magic arts	those who practise sorceries (magic arts)
Good News for Modern Man	witchcraft	magic	false magic	those who practice magic	those who practice magic

or drug-sorcery, and you render this word as sorcery-in-general, you have buried the drug implication among so many other implications that you have effectively lost it. The end result is a gross mistranslation and eclipse of the original and primary message.

More recently there has arisen a final confusion which has *totally* obliterated the meaning of the five New Testament passages containing the *pharmak* root words. This difficulty did not obtain for the English-speaking people who read the King James Version in the seventeenth century, but it overwhelmingly affects most modern readers of English-language Bibles. Sorcery by definition involves evil spirits, and most moderns cannot possibly take sorcery—drug-sorcery or any other kind of sorcery—as a real problem since they do not believe in evil spirits. So you end up with the absurdity of a solemn biblical warning against what *must* seem to a modern man an unreal, fairy-tale practice.

The Bible, along with all of the other great spiritual documents of mankind, really does present us with a problem, in that it so manifestly and unanimously asserts the reality of evil spirits. Christ dealt directly with the reality of evil spirits. He conversed with them and practiced healing by casting them out. Paul and John believed in evil spirits. As late as 1611, most of the population, including the committee of scholars who produced the King James Version of the Bible, believed in evil spirits. But not many twentieth century men and women do. Not many *can.*

There is now, however, good reason to suspect that Christ was right about evil spirits and that conventional, secular modern thinking (by which every one of us is deeply influenced, whether we will or no) is mistaken. The hair-raising testimonies of many who have practiced drug-sorcery on themselves with psychedelics, narcotics, and other mind-changers have provided impressive corroboration for the view that Christ was on target and that the post-"enlightenment" rationalists were mistaken in this matter of the existence of evil spirits.

We modern men are the victims of *negative superstition*. We deny the reality of dangerous and frightening beings which are utterly real and closely related to us but which we are unable to see or to sense simply because we have lost the spiritual faculties to do so. We cannot deprive these beings of power by a mere infantile refusal to acknowledge their existence. We end up experiencing their effects in the guise of "inexplicable" obstructions, reversals, mental and physical illnesses, and calamities. We render ourselves incapable of countering their influence when we remain ignorant of the nature, the habits, and the very presence of these our preternatural enemies.

But the problem goes deeper. It is not just evil spirits that we moderns tend to disbelieve in. It is *spirit in any form*. We gag on angels as hard as we gag on demons. The highest order of reality that we deign to deal with is the human mind, and we are not very comfortable or very capable in dealing with that.

Unfortunately, evil spirits are frequently cleverer and stronger than human mental processes. They are able to subvert thought, unless the people doing the thinking are protected by a higher influence, an extra-mental reality which is also Spirit, specifically the benign Spirit who rules the universe, God.

Pharmakeia—drugging, or drug-sorcery—is warned against so strongly in the New Testament precisely because it subjects men to possession by evil spirits as only a few other sins, like murder and adultery, do.

For a person who has corrupted himself by the practice of *pharmakeia*, however, the New Testament provides more than just a threat of consuming fire. For the repentant—those who sincerely wish to change—it indicates the way out of the drug trap. Instead of submitting to seduction by evil spirits through the use of mind-altering drugs, it teaches us how to submit to Spirit, to God, through surrender of our self-will, through prayer, and through a life of service and testimony to the way out, which is the Way, which is Christ.

WHY DO MEN
STUPEFY THEMSELVES?

What is the explanation of the fact that people use things that stupefy them: vodka, wine, beer, hashish, opium, tobacco, and other things less common: ether, morphia, fly agaric, etc.? Why did the practice begin? Why has it spread so rapidly, and why is it still spreading among all sorts of people, savage and civilized? How is it that where there is no vodka, wine or beer, we find opium, hashish, fly agaric, and the like, and that tobacco is used everywhere?

Why do people wish to stupefy themselves?

Ask anyone why he began drinking wine and why he now drinks it. He will reply, "Oh, I like it, and everybody drinks," and he may add, "it cheers me up." Some—those who have never once taken the trouble to consider whether they do well or ill to drink wine—may add that

39

wine is good for the health and adds to one's strength; that is to say, will make a statement long since proved baseless.

Ask a smoker why he began to use tobacco and why he now smokes, and he also will reply: "To while away the time; everybody smokes."

Similar answers would probably be given by those who use opium, hashish, morphia, or fly-agaric.

"To while away time, to cheer oneself up; everybody does it." But it might be excusable to twiddle one's thumbs, to whistle, to hum tunes, to play a fife or to do something of that sort "to while away the time," "to cheer oneself up," or "because everybody does it"—that is to say, it might be excusable to do something which does not involve wasting Nature's wealth, or spending what has cost great labor to produce, or doing what brings evident harm to oneself and to others. But to produce tobacco, wine, hashish, and opium, the labor of millions of men is spent, and millions and millions of acres of the best land (often amid a population that is short of land) are employed to grow potatoes, hemp, poppies, vines, and tobacco.

Moreover, the use of these evidently harmful things produces terrible evils known and admitted by everyone, and destroys more people than all the wars and contagious diseases added together. And people know this, so that they cannot really use these things "to while away time," "to cheer themselves up," or because "everybody does it."

There must be some other reason.

Continually and everywhere one meets people who love their children and are ready to make all kinds of sacrifices for them, but who yet spend on vodka, wine and beer, or on opium, hashish, or even tobacco, as much as would quite suffice to feed their hungry and poverty-stricken children, or at least as much as would suffice to save them from misery.

Evidently if a man who has to choose between the want and sufferings of a family he loves on the one hand, and abstinence from stupefying things on the other, chooses the former—he must be induced thereto by something more potent than the consideration that everybody does it, or that it is pleasant. Evidently it is done not "to while away time," nor merely "to cheer himself up." He is actuated by some more powerful cause.

This cause—as far as I have detected it by reading about this subject and by observing other people, and particularly by observing my own case when I used to drink wine and smoke tobacco—this cause, I think, may be explained as follows:

When observing his own life, a man may often notice in himself two different beings: the one is blind and physical, the other sees and is spiritual. The blind animal being eats, drinks, rests, sleeps, propagates, and moves, like a wound-up machine. The seeing, spiritual being that is bound up with the animal does nothing of itself, but only appraises the activity of the animal being; coinciding with it when approving its activity, and diverging from it when disapproving.

This observing being may be compared to the needle of a compass, pointing with one end to the north and with the other to the south, but screened along its whole length by something not noticeable so long as it and the needle both point the same way; but which becomes obvious as soon as they point different ways.

In the same manner the seeing, spiritual being, whose manifestation we commonly call conscience, always points with one end towards right and with the other towards wrong, and we do not notice it while we follow the course it shows: the course from wrong to right. But one

need only do something contrary to the indication of conscience to become aware of this spiritual being, which then shows how the animal activity has diverged from the direction indicated by conscience.

And as a navigator conscious that he is on the wrong track cannot continue to work the oars, engine, or sails, till he has adjusted his course to the indications of the compass, or has obliterated his consciousness of this divergence—each man who has felt the duality of his animal activity and his conscience can continue his activity only by adjusting that activity to the demands of conscience, or by hiding from himself the indications conscience gives him of the wrongness of his animal life.

All human life, we may say, consists solely of these two activities: (1) bringing one's activities into harmony with conscience, or (2) hiding from oneself the indications of conscience in order to be able to continue to live as before.

Some do the first, others the second. To attain the first there is but one means: moral enlightenment—the increase of light in oneself and attention to what it shows. To attain the second—to hide from oneself the indications of conscience—there are two means: one external and the other internal. The external means consists in occupations that divert one's attention from the indications given by conscience; the internal method consists in darkening conscience itself.

As a man has two ways of avoiding seeing an object that is before him: either by diverting his sight to other more striking objects, or by obstructing the sight of his own eyes—just so a man can hide from himself the indications of conscience in two ways: either by the external method of diverting his attention to various occupations, cares, amusements, or games; or by the internal method of obstructing the organ of attention itself.

For people of dull, limited moral feeling, the external diversions are often quite sufficient to enable them not to perceive the indications conscience gives of the wrongness of their lives. But for morally sensitive people those means are often insufficient.

The external means do not quite divert attention from the consciousness of discord between one's life and the demands of conscience. This consciousness hampers one's life: and in order to be able to go on living as before people have recourse to the reliable, internal method, which is that of darkening conscience itself by poisoning the brain with stupefying substances.

One is not living as conscience demands, yet lacks the strength to reshape one's life in accord with its demands. The diversions which might distract attention from the consciousness of this discord are insufficient, or have become stale, and so—in order to be able to live on, disregarding the indications conscience gives of the wrongness of their life—people (by poisoning it temporarily) stop the activity of the organ through which conscience manifests itself, as a man by covering his eyes hides from himself what he does not wish to see.

The cause of the world-wide consumption of hashish, opium, wine, and tobacco, lies not in the taste, nor in any pleasure, recreation, or mirth they afford, but simply in man's need to hide from himself the demands of conscience.

I was going along the street one day, and passing some cabmen who were talking, I heard one of them say: "Of course when a man's sober he's ashamed to do it!"

When a man is sober he is ashamed of what seems all right when he is drunk. In these words we have the essential underlying cause prompting men to resort to stupefiers. People resort to them either to escape feeling ashamed after having done something contrary to their consciences, or to bring themselves beforehand into a state in which they can commit actions contrary to conscience, but to which their animal nature prompts them.

A man when sober is ashamed to go after a prostitute, ashamed to steal, ashamed to kill. A drunken man is ashamed of none of these things, and therefore if a man wishes to do something his conscience condemns he stupefies himself.

I remember being struck by the evidence of a cook who was tried for murdering a relation of mine, an old lady in whose service he lived. He related that when he had sent away his paramour, the servant-girl, and the time had come to act, he wished to go into the bedroom with a knife, but felt that while sober he could not commit the deed he had planned . . . "when a man's sober he's ashamed." He turned back, drank two tumblers of vodka he had prepared beforehand, and only then felt himself ready, and committed the crime.

Nine-tenths of the crimes are committed in that way: "Drink to keep up your courage."

Half the women who fall do so under the influence of wine. Nearly all visits to disorderly houses are paid by men who are intoxicated. People know this capacity of wine to stifle the voice of conscience, and intentionally use it for that purpose.

Not only do people stupefy themselves to stifle their own consciences, but, knowing how wine acts, they intentionally stupefy others when they wish to make them commit actions contrary to conscience—that is, they arrange to stupefy people in order to deprive them of conscience. In war, soldiers are usually intoxicated before a hand-to-hand fight. All the French soldiers in the assaults on Sevastopol were drunk.

When a fortified place has been captured but the soldiers do not sack it and slay the defenseless old men and children, orders are often given to make them drunk and then they do what is expected of them.

Everyone knows people who have taken to drink in consequence of some wrong-doing that has tormented their conscience. Anyone can notice that those who lead immoral lives are more attracted than others by stupefying substances. Bands of robbers or thieves, and prostitutes, cannot live without intoxicants.

Everyone knows and admits that the use of stupefying substances is a consequence of the pangs of conscience, and that in certain immoral ways of life stupefying substances are employed to stifle conscience. Everyone knows and admits also that the use of stupefiers does stifle conscience: that a drunken man is capable of deeds of which when sober he would not think for a moment.

Everyone agrees to this, but strange to say when the use of stupefiers does not result in such deeds as thefts, murders, violations, and so forth—when stupefiers are taken not after some terrible crimes, but by men following professions which we do not consider criminal, and when the substances are consumed not in large quantities at once but continually in moderate doses—then (for some reason) it is assumed that stupefying substances have no tendency to stifle conscience.

Thus it is supposed that a well-to-do Russian's glass of vodka before each meal and tumbler of wine with the meal, or a Frenchman's absinthe, or an Englishman's port wine and porter, or a German's lager-beer, or a well-to-do Chinaman's moderate dose of opium, and the smoking of tobacco with them—is done only for pleasure and has no effect whatever on these people's consciences.

It is supposed that if after this customary stupefaction no crime is committed—no theft or murder, but only customary bad and stupid actions—then these actions have occurred of themselves and are not evoked by the stupefaction. It is supposed that if these people have not committed offences against the criminal law they have no need to stifle the voice of conscience, and that the life led by people who habitually stupefy themselves is quite a good life, and would be precisely the same if they did not stupefy themselves. It is supposed that the constant use of stupefiers does not in the least darken their consciences.

Though everybody knows by experience that a man's frame of mind is altered by the use of wine or tobacco, that he is not ashamed of things which but for the stimulant he would be ashamed of, that after each twinge of conscience, however slight, he is inclined to have recourse to some stupefier, and that under the influence of stupefiers it is difficult to reflect on his life and position, and that the constant and regular use of stupefiers produces the same physiological effect as its occasional immoderate use does—yet in spite of all this it seems to men who drink and smoke moderately that they use stupefiers not at all to stifle conscience, but only for the flavor or for pleasure.

But one need only think of the matter seriously and impartially—not trying to excuse oneself—to understand, first, that if the use of stupefiers in large occasional doses stifles man's conscience, their regular use must have a like effect (always first intensifying and then dulling the activity of the brain) whether they are taken in large or small doses; secondly, that all stupefiers have the quality of stifling conscience, and have this always—both when under their influence murders, robberies, and violations are committed, and when under their influence words are spoken which would not have been spoken, or things are thought and felt which but for them would not have been thought and felt; and, thirdly, that if the use of stupefiers is needed to pacify and stifle the consciences of thieves, robbers, and prostitutes, it is also wanted by people engaged in occupations condemned by their own consciences, even though these occupations may be considered proper and honorable by other people.

In a word, it is impossible to avoid understanding that the use of stupefiers, in large or small amounts, occasionally or regularly, in the higher or lower circles of society, is evoked by one and the same cause, the need to

When the ruler drinks, the subjects get out of hand (following page). It is no mistake, no mere oddity of design, that the King is at the precise center of this picture. He represents the *conscious individual*, the central intelligence in each of us. All of the surrounding characters are our physical functions and psychic appetites. Every human being was meant to be the monarch of his own body and soul, but he can be so only when he is truly conscious, "in full possession of all his faculties."

When, instead, the king stupefies himself with the heady wine of egotism—arrogating the supreme authority of God to himself—the servant members of his body and soul are free to run riot. The dissolute and powerless condition of an actual drunkard is a caricature on the physical level of this spiritual subversion. It is no accident that the use and abuse of stupefying drugs everywhere accompanies a turning away from God and from the claims of conscience.

There are other ways to look at this picture, which is clearly a product of the teaching of a School of the Way: For example, the King is Observing I (of Gurdjieff's system), the first phase and function of an entity which, in a fully developed human being, will reunite with Real I, the Self, the Master. While the King remains alert and unidentified with his subjects, all is well, and order prevails in the monarchy; but when he drinks, literally or figuratively, he falls into identification with the boisterous rabble of I's that is his personality. And so, for the duration of his "drunken sleep," he loses the majesty—the right and effective power to command—that was his birthright.

stifle the voice of conscience in order not to be aware of the discord existing between one's way of life and the demands of one's conscience.

In that alone lies the reason of the widespread use of all stupefying substances, and among the rest of tobacco—probably the most generally used and most harmful.

It is supposed that tobacco cheers one up, clears the thoughts, and attracts one merely like any other habit—without at all producing the deadening of conscience produced by wine.

But you need only observe attentively the conditions under which a special desire to smoke arises, and you will be convinced that stupefying with tobacco acts on the conscience as wine does, and that people consciously have recourse to this method of stupefaction just when they require it for that purpose. If tobacco merely cleared the thoughts and cheered one up there would not be such a passionate craving for it, a craving showing itself just on certain definite occasions. People would not say, as they do, that they would rather go without bread than without tobacco, and would not often actually prefer tobacco to food.

That cook who murdered his mistress said that when he entered the bedroom and had gashed her throat with his knife and she had fallen with a rattle in her throat and the blood had gushed out in a torrent—he lost his courage. "I could not finish her off," he said, "but I went back from the bedroom to the sitting-room and sat down there and smoked a cigarette." Only after stupefying himself with tobacco was he able to return to the bedroom, finish cutting the old lady's throat, and begin examining her things.

Evidently the desire to smoke at that moment was evoked in him, not by a wish to clear his thoughts or be merry, but by the need to stifle something that prevented him from completing what he had planned to do.

Any smoker may detect in himself the same definite desire to stupefy himself with tobacco at certain specially difficult moments. I look back at the days when I used to smoke: when was it that I felt a special need of tobacco? It was always at moments when I did not wish to remember certain things that presented themselves to my recollection, when I wished to forget—not to think.

I sit by myself doing nothing and know I ought to set to work, but I don't feel inclined to, so I smoke and go on sitting. I have promised to be at someone's house by five o'clock, but I have stayed too long somewhere else. I remember that I have missed the appointment, but I do not like to remember it, so I smoke. I get vexed and say unpleasant things to someone, and know I am doing wrong and see that I ought to stop, but I want to give vent to my irritability—so I smoke and continue to be irritable. I play at cards and lose more than I intended to risk—so I smoke. I have placed myself in an awkward position, have acted badly, have made a mistake, and ought to acknowledge the mess I am in and thus escape from it, but I do not like to acknowledge it, so I accuse others—and smoke. I write something and am not quite satisfied with what I have written. I ought to abandon it, but I wish to finish what I have planned to do—so I smoke. I dispute, and see that my opponent and I do not understand and cannot understand one another, but I wish to express my opinion, so I continue to talk—and I smoke.

What distinguishes tobacco from most other stupefiers, besides the ease with which one can stupefy oneself with it and its apparent harmlessness, is its portability and the possibility of applying it to meet small, isolated occurrences that disturb one.

Not to mention that the use of opium, wine, and hash-

ish involves the use of certain appliances not always at hand, while one can always carry tobacco and paper with one; and that the opium-smoker and the drunkard evoke horror while a tobacco-smoker does not seem at all repulsive—the advantage of tobacco over other stupefiers is, that the stupefaction of opium, hashish, or wine extends to all the sensations and acts received or produced during a certain somewhat extended period of time—while the stupefaction from tobacco can be directed to any separate occurrence.

You wish to do what you ought not to, so you smoke a cigarette and stupefy yourself sufficiently to enable you to do what should not be done, and then you are all right again, and can think and speak clearly; or you feel you have done what you should not—again you smoke a cigarette and the unpleasant consciousness of the wrong or awkward action is obliterated, and you can occupy yourself with other things and forget it.

But apart from individual cases in which every smoker has recourse to smoking, not to satisfy a habit or while away time but as a means of stifling his conscience with reference to acts he is about to commit or has already committed, is it not quite evident that there is a strict and definite relation between men's way of life and their passion for smoking?

When do lads begin to smoke? Usually when they lose their childish innocence. How is it that smokers can abandon smoking when they come among more moral conditions of life, and again start smoking as soon as they fall among a depraved set? Why do gamblers almost all smoke? Why among women do those who lead a regular life smoke least? Why do prostitutes and madmen *all* smoke?

Habit is habit, but evidently smoking stands in some definite connection with the craving to stifle conscience, and achieves the end required of it.

One may observe in the case of almost every smoker to what an extent smoking drowns the voice of conscience. Every smoker when yielding to his desire forgets, or sets at naught, the very first demands of social life—demands he expects others to observe, and which he observes in all other cases until his conscience is stifled by tobacco. Everyone of average education considers it inadmissible, ill-bred, and inhumane to infringe the peace, comfort, and still more the health of others for his own pleasure. No one would allow himself to wet a room in which people are sitting, or to make a noise, shout, let in cold, hot, or ill-smelling air, or commit acts that incommode or harm others. But out of a thousand smokers not one will shrink from producing unwholesome smoke in a room where the air is breathed by non-smoking women and children.

If smokers do usually say to those present: "You don't object?" everyone knows that the customary answer is: "Not at all" (although it cannot be pleasant to a non-smoker to breathe tainted air, and to find stinking cigar ends in glasses and cups or on plates and candlesticks, òr even in ashpans). But even if non-smoking adults did not object to tobacco smoke, it could not be pleasant or good for the children whose consent no one asks. Yet people who are honorable and humane in all other respects smoke in the presence of children at dinner in small rooms, vitiating the air with tobacco smoke, without feeling the slightest twinge of conscience.

It is usually said (and I used to say) that smoking facilitates mental work. And that is undoubtedly true if one considers only the quantity of one's mental output. To a man who smokes, and who consequently ceases strictly to appraise and weigh his thoughts, it seems as if he suddenly had many thoughts. But this is not because he really has many thoughts, but only because he has lost control of his thoughts.

When a man works he is always conscious of two beings in himself: the one works, the other appraises the work. The stricter the appraisement the slower and the better is the work; and vice versa, when the appraiser is under the influence of something that stupefies him, more work gets done, but its quality is poorer.

"If I do not smoke I cannot write. I cannot get on; I begin and cannot continue," is what is usually said, and what I used to say. What does it really mean? It means either that you have nothing to write, or that what you wish to write has not yet matured in your consciousness but is only beginning dimly to present itself to you, and the appraising critic within, when not stupefied with tobacco, tells you so. If you did not smoke you would either abandon what you have begun, or you would wait until your thought has cleared itself in your mind; you would try to penetrate into what presents itself dimly to you, would consider the objections that offer themselves, and would turn all your attention to the elucidation of the thought.

But you smoke, the critic within you is stupefied, and the hindrance to your work is removed. What seemed insignificant to you when not inebriated by tobacco, again seems important; what seemed obscure no longer seems so; the objections that presented themselves vanish and you continue to write, and write much and rapidly.

But can such a small—such a trifling—alteration as the slight intoxication produced by the moderate use of wine or tobacco produce important consequences?

"If a man smokes opium or hashish, or intoxicates himself with wine till he falls down and loses his senses, of course the consequences may be very serious; but it surely cannot have any serious consequences if a man merely comes slightly under the influence of hops or tobacco,'' is what is usually said.

It seems to people that a slight stupefaction, a little darkening of the judgment, cannot have any important influence. But to think so is like supposing that it may harm a watch to be struck against a stone, but that a little dirt introduced into it cannot be harmful.

Remember, however, that the chief work actuating man's whole life is not done by his hands, his feet, or his back, but by his consciousness. Before a man can do anything with his feet or hands, a certain alteration has first to take place in his consciousness. And this alteration defines all the subsequent movements of the man. Yet these alterations are always minute and almost imperceptible.

Bryullov [a celebrated Russian painter] one day corrected a pupil's study. The pupil, having glanced at the altered drawing, exclaimed: "Why, you only touched it a tiny bit, but it is quite another thing." Bryullov replied: "Art begins where the tiny bit begins."

That saying is strikingly true not only of art but of all life. One may say that true life begins where the tiny bit begins—where what seem to us minute and infinitely small alterations take place. True life is not lived where great external changes take place—where people move about, clash, fight, and slay one another—it is lived only where these tiny, tiny, infinitesimally small changes occur.

Raskolnikov [the hero of Dostoevsky's novel, *Crime and Punishment*] did not live his true life when he murdered the old woman or her sister. When murdering the old woman herself, and still more when murdering her sister, he did not live his true life, but acted like a machine, doing what he could not help doing—discharging the cartridge with which he had long been loaded. One

old woman was killed, another stood before him, the axe was in his hand.

Raskolnikov lived his true life not when he met the old woman's sister, but at the time when he had not yet killed any old woman, nor entered a stranger's lodging with intent to kill, nor held the axe in his hand, nor had the loop in his overcoat by which the axe hung.

He lived his true life when he was lying on the sofa in his room, deliberating not at all about the old woman, nor even as to whether it is or is not permissible at the will of one man to wipe from the face of the earth another, unnecessary and harmful, man, but whether he ought to live in Petersburg or not, whether he ought to accept money from his mother or not, and on other questions not at all relating to the old woman. And then —in that region quite independent of animal activities— the question whether he would or would not kill the old woman was decided. That question was decided—not when, having killed one old woman, he stood before another, axe in hand—but when he was doing nothing and was only thinking, when only his consciousness was active: and in that consciousness tiny, tiny alterations were taking place.

It is at such times that one needs the greatest clearness to decide correctly the questions that have arisen, and it is just then that one glass of beer, or one cigarette, may prevent the solution of the question, may postpone the decision, stifle the voice of conscience and prompt a decision of the question in favor of the lower, animal nature—as was the case with Raskolnikov.

Tiny, tiny alterations—but on them depend the most immense and terrible consequences. Many material changes may result from what happens when a man has taken a decision and begun to act: houses, riches, and people's bodies may perish, but nothing more important can happen than what was hidden in the man's consciousness. The limits of what can happen are set by consciousness.

And boundless results of unimaginable importance may follow from most minute alterations occurring in the domain of consciousness.

Do not let it be supposed that what I am saying has anything to do with the question of free will or determinism. Discussion on that question is superfluous for my purpose, or for any other for that matter. Without deciding the question whether a man can, or cannot, act as he wishes (a question in my opinion not correctly stated), I am merely saying that since human activity is conditioned by infinitesimal alterations in consciousness, it follows (no matter whether we admit the existence of free will or not) that we must pay particular attention to the condition in which these minute alterations take place, just as one must be specially attentive to the condition of scales on which other things are to be weighed.

We must, as far as it depends on us, try to put ourselves and others in conditions which will not disturb the clearness and delicacy of thought necessary for the correct working of conscience, and must not act in the contrary manner—trying to hinder and confuse the work of conscience by the use of stupefying substances.

For man is a spiritual as well as an animal being.

He may be moved by things that influence his spiritual nature, or by things that influence his animal nature, as a clock may be moved by its hands or by its main wheel. And just as it is best to regulate the movement of a clock by means of its inner mechanism, so a man—oneself or another—is best regulated by means of his consciousness. And as with a clock one has to take special care of that part by means of which one can best move the inner mechanism, so with a man one must take special care of

the cleanness and clearness of consciousness which is the thing that best moves the whole man.

To doubt this is impossible; everyone knows it. But a need to deceive oneself arises. People are not as anxious that consciousness should work correctly as they are that it should seem to them that what they are doing is right, and they deliberately make use of substances that disturb the proper working of their consciousness.

People drink and smoke, not casually, not from dullness, not to cheer themselves up, not because it is pleasant, but in order to drown the voice of conscience in themselves. And in that case, how terrible must be the consequences! Think what a building would be like erected by people who did not use a straight plumb-rule to get the walls perpendicular, nor right-angled squares to get the corners correct, but used a soft rule which would bend to suit all irregularities in the walls, and a square that expanded to fit any angle, acute or obtuse.

Yet, thanks to self-stupefaction, that is just what is being done in life. Life does not accord with conscience, so conscience is made to bend to life.

This is done in the life of individuals, and it is done in the life of humanity as a whole, which consists of the lives of individuals.

To grasp the full significance of such stupefying of one's consciousness, let each one carefully recall the spiritual conditions he has passed through at each period of his life. Everyone will find that at each period of his life certain moral questions confronted him which he ought to solve, and on the solution of which the whole welfare of his life depended. For the solution of these questions great concentration of attention was needful. Such concentration of attention is a labor. In every labor, especially at the beginning, there is a time when the work seems difficult and painful, and when human weakness prompts a desire to abandon it. Physical work seems painful at first; mental work still more so. As Lessing says: people are inclined to cease to think at the point at which thought begins to be difficult; but it is just there, I would add, that thinking begins to be fruitful.

A man feels that to decide the questions confronting him needs labor—often painful labor—and he wishes to evade this. If he had no means of stupefying his faculties he could not expel from his consciousness the questions that confront him, and the necessity of solving them would be forced upon him. But man finds that there exists a means to drive off these questions whenever they present themselves—and he uses it.

As soon as the questions awaiting solution begin to torment him he has recourse to these means, and avoids the disquietude evoked by the troublesome questions. Consciousness ceases to demand their solution, and the unsolved questions remain unsolved till his next period of enlightenment.

But when that period comes the same thing is repeated, and the man goes on for months, years, or even for his whole life, standing before those same moral questions and not moving a step towards their solution. Yet it is in the solution of moral questions that life's whole movement consists.

What occurs is as if a man who needs to see to the bottom of some muddy water to obtain a precious pearl, but who dislikes entering the water, should stir it up each time it begins to settle and become clear. Many a man continues to stupefy himself all his life long, and remains immovable at the same once-accepted, obscure, self-contradictory view of life—pressing, as each period of enlightenment approaches, ever at one and the same wall against which he pressed ten or twenty years ago, and which he cannot break through because he intentionally blunts that sharp point of thought which alone could pierce it.

Let each man remember himself as he has been during the years of his drinking or smoking, and let him test the matter in his experience of other people, and everyone will see a definite constant line dividing those who are addicted to stupefiers from those who are free from them. The more a man stupefies himself the more he is morally immovable.

Terrible, as they are described to us, are the consequences of opium and hashish on individuals; terrible, as we know them, are the consequences of alcohol to flagrant drunkards; but incomparably more terrible to our whole society are the consequences of what is considered the harmless, moderate use of spirits, wine, beer, and tobacco, to which the majority of men, and especially our so-called cultured classes, are addicted.

The consequences must naturally be terrible, admitting the fact, which must be admitted, that the guiding activities of society—political, official, scientific, literary, and artistic—are carried on for the most part by people in an abnormal state: by people who are drunk.

It is generally supposed that a man who, like most people of our well-to-do-classes, takes alcoholic drink almost every time he eats, is in a perfectly normal and sober condition next day, during working hours. But this is quite an error. A man who drank a bottle of wine, a glass of spirits, or two glasses of ale, yesterday, is now in the usual state of drowsiness or depression which follows excitement, and is therefore in a condition of mental prostration, which is increased by smoking. For a man who habitually smokes and drinks in moderation, to bring his brain into a normal condition would require at least a week or more of abstinence from wine and tobacco. But that hardly ever occurs.

Why Do Men Stupefy Themselves?

So that most of what goes on among us, whether done by people who rule and teach others, or by those who are ruled and taught, is done when the doers are not sober.*

And let not this be taken as a joke or an exaggeration. The confusion, and above all the imbecility, of our lives, arises chiefly from the constant state of intoxication in which most people live. Could people who are not drunk possibly do all that is being done around us—from building the Eiffel Tower to accepting military service?

Without any need whatever, a company is formed, capital collected, men labor, make calculations, and draw plans; millions of working days and thousands of tons of iron are spent to build a tower; and millions of people consider it their duty to climb up it, stop awhile on it, and then climb down again; and the building and visiting of this tower evoke no other reflection than a wish and intention to build other towers, in other places, still bigger. Could sober people act like that?

---

* But how is it that people who do not drink or smoke are often morally on an incomparably lower plane than others who drink and smoke? And why do people who drink and smoke often manifest very high qualities both mentally and morally?

The answer is, first, that we do not know the height that those who drink and smoke would have attained had they not drunk and smoked.

And secondly, from the fact that morally gifted people achieve great things in spite of the deteriorating effect of stupefying substances, we can but conclude that they would have produced yet greater things had they not stupefied themselves. It is very probable, as a friend remarked to me, that Kant's works would not have been written in such a curious and bad style had he not smoked so much.

Lastly, the lower a man's mental and moral plane the less does he feel the discord between his conscience and his life, and therefore the less does he feel a craving to stupefy himself; and on the other hand a parallel reason explains why the most sensitive natures—those which immediately and morbidly feel the discord between life and conscience—so often indulge in narcotics and perish by them.

Or take another case. For dozens of years past, all the European peoples have been busy devising the very best ways of killing people, and teaching as many young men as possible, as soon as they reach manhood, how to murder. Everyone knows that there can be no invasion by barbarians, but that these preparations made by the different civilized and Christian nations are directed against one another; everyone knows that this is burdensome, painful, inconvenient, ruinous, immoral, impious, and irrational—but everyone continues to prepare for mutual murder. Some devise political combinations to decide who is to kill whom and with what allies, others direct those who are being taught to murder, and others again yield—against their will, against their conscience, against their reason—to these preparations for murder.

Could sober people do these things? Only drunkards who never reach a state of sobriety could do them and live on in the horrible state of discord between life and conscience in which, not only in this but in all other respects, the people of our society are now living.

Never before, I suppose, have people lived with the demands of their conscience so evidently in contradiction to their actions.

Humanity today has as it were stuck fast. It is as though some external cause hindered it from occupying a position in natural accord with its perceptions. And the cause—if not the only one, then certainly the greatest—is this physical condition of stupefaction induced by wine and tobacco to which the great majority of people in our society reduce themselves.

Emancipation from this terrible evil will be an epoch in the life of humanity; and that epoch seems to be at hand. The evil is recognized. An alteration has already taken place in our perception concerning the use of stupefying substances. People have understood the

70

terrible harm of these things and are beginning to point them out, and this almost unnoticed alteration in perception will inevitably bring about the emancipation of men from the use of stupefying things—will enable them to open their eyes to the demands of their consciences, and they will begin to order their lives in accord with their perceptions.

And this seems to be already beginning. But as always it is beginning among the upper classes only after all the lower classes have already been infected.

THE FIRST STEP

If a man is working in order to accomplish whatever he has in hand and not merely making a pretence of work, his actions will necessarily follow one another in a certain sequence determined by the nature of the work. If he postpones to a later time what from the nature of the work should be done first, or if he altogether omits some essential part, he is certainly not working seriously but only pretending.

This rule holds unalterably true whether the work be physical or not. As a man seriously wishing to bake bread first kneads the flour and then heats the brick-oven, sweeps out the ashes, and so on, so also a man seriously wishing to lead a good life adopts a certain order of succession in the attainment of the necessary qualities.

This rule is especially important in regard to right living; for whereas in the case of physical work, such as making bread, it is easy to discover by the result whether a man is seriously engaged in work or only pretending, no such verification is possible in regard to goodness of life.

If without kneading the dough or heating the oven people merely pretend to make bread—as they do in the theater—then the absence of bread makes it obvious that they were only pretending; but when a man pretends to be leading a good life we have no such direct indications that he is not striving seriously but only pretending, for not only are the results of a good life not always evident and palpable to those around, but very often such results even appear to them harmful. Respect for a man's activity and the acknowledgement of its utility and pleasantness by his contemporaries furnish no proof of the real goodness of his life.

Therefore, to distinguish the reality from the mere appearance of a good life, the indication given by a regular order of succession in the acquirement of the essential qualities is especially valuable. And this indication is valuable, not so much to enable us to discover the seriousness of other men's strivings after goodness as to test this sincerity in ourselves, for in this respect we are liable to deceive ourselves even more than we deceive others.

A correct order of succession in the attainment of virtues is an indispensable condition of advance towards a good life, and consequently the teachers of mankind have always prescribed a certain invariable order for their attainment.

All moral teachings set up that ladder which, as the Chinese wisdom has it, reaches from earth to heaven, and the ascent of which can only be accomplished by starting from the lowest step. As in the teaching of the Brahmins, Buddhists, Confucians, so also in the teaching of the Greek sages, steps were fixed, and a superior step could not be attained without the lower one having been previously taken. All the moral teachers of mankind, religious and non-religious alike, have admitted the necessity of a definite order of succession in the attainment of the qualities essential to a righteous life. The necessity for this sequence lies in the very essence of things, and therefore, it would seem, ought to be recognized by everyone.

But, strange to say, from the time Church-Christianity spread widely, the consciousness of this necessary order appears to have been more and more lost, and is now retained only among ascetics and monks.

Among worldly Christians it is taken for granted that the higher virtues may be attained not only in the absence of the lower ones, which are a necessary condition of the higher, but even in company with the greatest vices; and consequently the very conception of what constitutes a good life has reached a state of the greatest confusion in the minds of the majority of worldly people today.

In our times people have quite lost consciousness of the necessity of a sequence in the qualities a man must have to enable him to live a good life, and in consequence have lost the very conception of what constitutes a good life. This it seems to me has come about in the following way.

When Christianity replaced paganism it put forth moral demands superior to the heathen ones, and at the same time (as was also the case with pagan morality) it necessarily laid down an indispensable order for the attainment of virtues—certain steps to the attainment of a righteous life.

Plato's virtues, beginning with self-control, advanced through courage and wisdom to justice; the Christian virtues, commencing with self-renunciation, rise, through devotion to the will of God, to love.

Those who accepted Christianity seriously and strove to live righteous Christian lives, understood Christianity in this way, and always began living rightly by renouncing their lusts; which renunciation included the self-control of the pagans.

But let it not be supposed that Christianity in this matter was only echoing the teachings of paganism; let me not be accused of degrading Christianity from its lofty place to the level of heathenism. Such an accusation would be unjust, for I regard the Christian teaching as the highest the world has known, and as quite different from heathenism. Christian teaching replaced pagan teaching simply because the former was different from and superior to the latter. But both Christian and pagan teaching alike lead men toward truth and goodness; and as these are always the same, the way to them must also be the same, and the *first steps* on this way must inevitably be the same for Christian as for heathen.

The difference between the Christian and pagan teaching of goodness lies in this: that the heathen teaching is one of final perfection, while the Christian is one of infinite perfecting. Every heathen, non-Christian, teaching sets before men a model of final perfection; but the Christian teaching sets before them a model of infinite perfection. Plato, for instance, makes justice the model of perfection, whereas Christ's model is the infinite perfection of love. *"Be ye perfect, even as your Father in heaven is perfect."*

In this lies the difference, and from this results the different relation of pagan and Christian teaching towards different grades of virtue. According to the former the attainment of the highest virtue was possible, and each step towards this attainment had its comparative merit—

the higher the step the greater the merit; so that from the pagan point of view men may be divided into moral and immoral, into more or less immoral—whereas according to the Christian teaching, which sets up the ideal of infinite perfection, this division is impossible. There can be neither higher nor lower grades. In the Christian teaching, which shows the infinity of perfection, all steps are equal in relation to the infinite ideal.

Among the pagans the plane of virtue attained by a man constituted his merit; in Christianity merit consists only in the process of attaining, in the greater or lesser speed of attainment. From the pagan point of view a man who possessed the virtue of reasonableness stood morally higher than one deficient in that virtue, a man who in addition to reasonableness possessed courage stood higher still, a man who to reasonableness and courage added justice stood yet higher.

But one Christian cannot be regarded as morally either higher or lower than another. A man is more or less of a Christian only in proportion to the speed with which he advances towards infinite perfection, irrespective of the stage he may have reached at a given moment. Hence the stationary righteousness of the Pharisee was worth less than the progress of the repentant thief on the cross.

Such is the difference between the Christian and the pagan teachings. Consequently the stages of virtue, as for instance self-control and courage, which in paganism constitute merit, constitute none whatever in Christianity. In this respect the teachings differ. But with regard to the fact that there can be no advance towards virtue, towards perfection, except by mounting the lowest steps, paganism and Christianity are alike: here there can be no difference.

The Christian, like the pagan, must commence the work of perfecting himself from the beginning—at the same step at which the heathen begins it, namely, self-control; just as a man who wishes to ascend a flight of stairs cannot avoid beginning at the first step. The only difference is that for the pagan, self-control itself constitutes a virtue; whereas for the Christian it is only part of that self-abnegation which is itself but an indispensable condition of all aspiration after perfection. Therefore the manifestation of true Christianity could not but follow the same path that had been indicated and followed by paganism.

But not all men have understood Christianity as an aspiration towards the perfection of the heavenly Father. The majority of people have regarded it as a teaching about salvation—that is, deliverance from sin by grace transmitted through the Church according to the Catholics and Greek Orthodox; by faith in the Redemption according to the Protestants, the Reformed Church, and the Calvinists; or by means of the two combined according to others.

And it is precisely this teaching that has destroyed the sincerity and seriousness of men's relation to the moral teaching of Christianity.

However much the representatives of these faiths may preach that these means of salvation do not hinder man in his aspiration after a righteous life but on the contrary contribute towards it—still, from certain assertions certain deductions necessarily follow, and no arguments can prevent men from making these deductions when once they have accepted the assertions from which they flow.

If a man believes that he can be saved through grace transmitted by the Church, or through the sacrifice of the Redemption, it is natural for him to think that efforts of his own to live a right life are unnecessary—the more so when he is told that even the hope that his efforts will make him better is a sin. Consequently a man who believes that there are means other than personal effort by which he may escape sin or its results, cannot strive with the same energy and seriousness as the man who knows no other means.

And not striving with perfect seriousness, and knowing of other means besides personal effort, a man will inevitably neglect the unalterable order of succession for the attainment of the good qualities necessary to a good life. And this has happened with the majority of those who profess Christianity.

The doctrine that personal effort is not necessary for the attainment of spiritual perfection by man, but that there are other means of acquiring it, caused a relaxation of efforts to live a good life and a neglect of the consecutiveness indispensable for such a life.

The great mass of those who accepted Christianity, accepting it only externally, took advantage of the substitution of Christianity for paganism to free themselves from the demands of the heathen virtues—no longer imposed on them as Christians—and to free themselves from all conflict with their animal nature.

The same thing happens with those who cease to believe in the teaching of the Church. They are like the believers just mentioned, only—instead of grace bestowed by the Church or through Redemption—they put forward some imaginary good work approved of by the majority of men, such as the service of science, art, or humanity; and in the name of this imaginary good work they liberate themselves from the consecutive attainment of the qualities necessary for a good life, and are satisfied with pretending, like men on the stage, to live a good life.

Those who fell away from paganism without embracing Christianity in its true significance, began to preach love for God and man apart from self-renunciation, and justice without self-control; that is to say, they preached the higher virtues while omitting the lower ones: they preached not the virtues themselves, but their semblance.

Some preach love of God and man without self-renunciation, and others preach humaneness—the service of humanity—without self-control. And as this teaching, while pretending to introduce man into higher moral regions, encourages his animal nature by liberating him from the most elementary demands of morality—long ago acknowledged by the heathens and not only not rejected but strengthened by true Christianity—it was readily accepted both by believers and unbelievers.

Only the other day the Pope's Encyclical on Socialism was published, in which, after a pretended refutation of the Socialist view of the wrongfulness of private property; it was plainly said: "No one is commanded to distribute to others that which is required for his own necessities and those of his household; nor even to give away what is reasonably required to keep up becomingly his condition in life; for no one ought to live unbecomingly." (This is from St. Thomas Aquinas, who says, Nullus enim inconvenienter vivere debet.) "But when necessity has been fairly supplied, and one's position fairly considered, it is a duty to give to the indigent out of that which is over. That which remaineth give alms."

Thus now preaches the head of the most widespread Church. Thus have preached all the Church teachers who considered salvation by works as insufficient. And together with this teaching of selfishness, which prescribes that you shall give to your neighbors only what you do not want yourself, they preach love, and recall with pathos Paul's celebrated words about love in the thirteenth chapter of the First Epistle to the Corinthians.

Notwithstanding that the Gospels overflow with demands for self-renunciation, with indications that self-renunciation is the first condition of Christian perfection; notwithstanding such clear expressions as: "Whosoever will not take up his cross . . . " "Whosoever hath not forsaken father and mother . . . " "Whosoever shall lose his life . . . "—people assure themselves and others that it is possible to love men without renouncing that to which one is accustomed, or even what one pleases to consider becoming for oneself.

So speak the Church people; and Freethinkers who reject not only the Church but also the Christian teaching, think, speak, write, and act, in just the same way. These men assure themselves and others that they can serve mankind and lead a good life without in the least diminishing their needs and without overcoming their lusts.

Men have thrown aside the pagan sequence of virtues; but, not assimilating the Christian teaching in its true significance, they have not accepted the Christian sequence and are left quite without guidance.

In olden times, when there was no Christian teaching, all the teachers of life, beginning with Socrates, regarded self-control— ἐγκράτεια or σωφροσύνη—as the first virtue of life; and it was understood that every virtue must begin with and pass through this one. It was clear that a man who had no self-control, who had developed an immense number of desires and had yielded himself up to them, could not lead a good life. It was evident that before a man could even think of disinterestedness and justice—to say nothing of generosity or love—he must learn to exercise control over himself.

According to our present ideas nothing of the sort is necessary. We are convinced that a man who has developed his desires to the climax reached in our society, a man who cannot live without satisfying the hundred unnecessary habits that enslave him, can yet lead an altogether moral and good life.

Looked at from any point of view: the lowest, utilitarian; the higher, pagan, which demands justice; and especially the highest, Christian, which demands love—it should surely be clear to everyone that a man who uses for his own pleasure (which he might easily forgo) the labor, often the painful labor, of others, behaves wrongly; and that this is the very first wrong he must cease to commit if he wishes to live a good life.

From the utilitarian point of view such conduct is bad, because as long as he forces others to work for him a man is always in an unstable position; he accustoms himself to the satisfaction of his desires and becomes enslaved by them, while those who work for him do so with hatred and envy and only await an opportunity to free themselves from the necessity of so working. Consequently such a man is always in danger of being left with deeply rooted habits which create demands he cannot satisfy.

From the point of view of justice such conduct is bad, because it is not well to employ for one's own pleasure the labor of other men who themselves cannot afford a hundredth part of the pleasures enjoyed by him for whom they labor.

From the point of view of Christian love it can hardly be necessary to prove that a man who loves others will give them his own labor rather than take the fruit of their labor from them for his own pleasure.

But these demands of utility, justice, and love, are altogether ignored by our modern society. With us the effort to limit our desires is regarded as neither the first nor even the last condition of a good life, but as altogether unnecessary.

On the contrary, according to the prevailing and most widely spread teaching of life today, the augmentation of one's wants is regarded as a desirable condition; as a sign of development, civilization, culture, and perfection. So-called educated people regard habits of comfort, that is, of effeminacy, as not only harmless but even good, indicating a certain moral elevation—as almost a virtue.

It is thought that the more the wants, and the more refined these wants, the better.

This is shown very clearly by the descriptive poetry, and even more so by the novels, of the last two centuries.

How are the heroes and heroines who represent the ideals of virtue portrayed?

In most cases the men who are meant to represent something noble and lofty—from Childe Harold down to the latest heroes of Feuillet, Trollope, or Maupassant—are simply depraved sluggards, consuming in luxury the labor of thousands, and themselves doing nothing useful for anybody. The heroines—the mistresses who in one way or another afford more or less delight to these men—are as idle as they, and are equally ready to consume the labor of others by their luxury.

I do not refer to the representations of really abstemious and industrious people one occasionally meets with in literature. I am speaking of the usual type that serves as an ideal to the masses: of the character that the majority of men and women are trying to resemble.

I remember the difficulty (inexplicable to me at the time) that I experienced when I wrote novels, a difficulty with which I contended and with which I know all novelists now contend who have even the dimmest conception of what constitutes real moral beauty—the difficulty of portraying a type taken from the upper classes as ideally good and kind, and at the same time true to life.

To be true to life, a description of a man or woman of the upper, educated classes must show him in his usual surroundings—that is, in luxury, physical idleness, and demanding much. From a moral point of view such a person is undoubtedly objectionable. But it is necessary

to represent this person in such a way that he may appear attractive. And novelists try to do so. I also tried.

And, strange to say, such a representation, making an immoral fornicator and murderer (duellist or soldier), an utterly useless, idly drifting, fashionable buffoon, appear attractive, does not require much art or effort. The readers of novels are for the most part exactly such men, and therefore readily believe that these Childe Harolds, Onegins, Messieurs de Camors, etc., are very excellent people.

Clear proof that the men of our time really do not admit pagan self-control and Christian self-renunciation to be good and desirable qualities, but on the contrary regard the augmentation of wants as good and elevated, is to be found in the education given to the vast majority of children in our society. Not only are they not trained to self-control, as among the pagans, or to the self-renunciation proper to Christians, but they are deliberately inoculated with habits of effeminacy, physical idleness, and luxury.

I have long wished to write a fairy tale of this kind:

A woman, wishing to revenge herself on one who has injured her, carries off her enemy's child, and going to a sorcerer asks him to teach her how she can most cruelly wreak her vengeance on the stolen infant, the only child of her enemy. The sorcerer bids her carry the child to a place he indicates, and assures her that a most terrible vengeance will result.

The wicked woman follows his advice; but, keeping an eye upon the child, is astonished to see that it is found and adopted by a wealthy, childless man. She goes to the sorcerer and reproaches him, but he bids her wait. The child grows up in luxury and effeminacy. The woman is perplexed, but again the sorcerer bids her wait. And at length the time comes when the wicked woman is not only satisfied but has even to pity her victim.

He grows up in the effeminacy and dissoluteness of wealth, and owing to his good nature is ruined. Then begins a sequence of physical sufferings, poverty, and humiliation, to which he is especially sensitive and against which he knows not how to contend. Aspirations towards a moral life—and the weakness of his effeminate body accustomed to luxury and idleness; vain struggles; lower and still lower decline; drunkenness to drown thought, then crime and insanity or suicide.

And, indeed, one cannot regard without terror the education of the children of the wealthy class in our day. Only the cruellest foe could, one would think, inoculate a child with those defects and vices which are now instilled into him by his parents, especially by mothers.

One is awestruck at the sight, and still more at the results of this, if only one knows how to discern what is taking place in the souls of the best of these children, so carefully ruined by their parents. Habits of effeminacy are instilled into them at a time when they do not yet understand their moral significance.

Not only is the habit of temperance and self-control neglected, but, contrary to the educational practice of Sparta and of the ancient world in general, this quality is altogether atrophied.

Not only is man not trained to work, and to all the qualities essential to fruitful labor—concentration of mind, strenuousness, endurance, enthusiasm for work, ability to repair what is spoiled, familiarity with fatigue, joy in attainment—but he is habituated to idleness and to contempt for all the products of labor: is taught to spoil, throw away, and again procure for money anything he fancies, without a thought of how things are made.

Man is deprived of the power of acquiring the primary virtue of reasonableness, indispensable for the attainment of all the others, and is let loose in a world where people preach and praise the loftly virtues of justice, the service of man, and love.

It is well if the youth be endowed with a morally feeble and obtuse nature, which does not detect the difference between make-believe and genuine goodness of life, and is satisfied with the prevailing mutual deception. If this be the case all goes apparently well, and such a man will sometimes quietly live on with his moral consciousness unawakened till death.

But it is not always thus, especially of late, now that the consciousness of the immorality of such life fills the air and penetrates the heart unsought. Frequently, and ever more frequently, it happens that there awakens a demand for real, unfeigned morality; and then begin a painful inner struggle and suffering which end but rarely in the triumph of the moral sentiment.

A man feels that his life is bad, that he must reform it from the very roots, and he tries to do so; but he is then attacked on all sides by those who have passed through a similar struggle and have been vanquished. They endeavor by every means to convince him that this reform is quite unnecessary: that goodness does not at all depend upon self-control and self-renunciation, that it is possible while addicting himself to gluttony, personal adornment, physical idleness, and even fornication, to be a perfectly good and useful man.

And the struggle in most cases terminates lamentably. Either the man, overcome by his weakness, yields to the general opinion, stifles the voice of conscience, distorts his reason to justify himself, and continues to lead the old dissipated life, assuring himself that it is redeemed by faith in the Redemption or the Sacraments, or by service to science, to the State, or to art; or else he struggles, suffers, and finally becomes insane or shoots himself.

It seldom happens, amid all the temptations that sur-
round him, that a man of our society understands what
was thousands of years ago, and still is, an elementary
truth for all reasonable people: namely, that for the attainment of a good life it is necessary first of all to cease
to live an evil life; that for the attainment of the higher
virtues it is needful first of all to acquire the virtue of
abstinence or self-control as the pagans called it, or of
self-renunciation as Christianity has it, and therefore it
seldom happens that he succeeds in attaining this primary virtue by gradual efforts.

I have just been reading the letters of one of our highly
educated and advanced men of the eighteen-forties, the
exile Ogaryev, to another yet more highly educated and
gifted man, Herzen.

In these letters Ogaryev gives expression to his sincere
thoughts and highest aspirations, and one cannot fail to
see that—as was natural to a young man—he rather
shows off before his friend. He talks of self-perfecting, of
sacred friendship, love, the service of science, of humanity, and the like. And at the same time he calmly writes
that he often irritates the companion of his life by "returning home in an unsober state, or disappearing for
many hours with a fallen, but dear creature. . . ." as he
expresses it.

Evidently it never even occurred to this remarkably
kindhearted, talented, and well-educated man that there
was anything at all objectionable in the fact that he, a
married man awaiting the confinement of his wife (in his
next letter he writes that his wife has given birth to a
child), returned home intoxicated and disappeared with
dissolute women. It did not enter his head that until he
had commenced the struggle and had at least to some
extent conquered his inclination to drunkenness and
fornication, he could not think of friendship and love

and still less of serving anyone or anything.

But he not only did not struggle against these vices—he evidently thought there was something very nice in them, and that they did not in the least hinder the struggle for perfection; and therefore instead of hiding them from the friend in whose eyes he wishes to appear in a good light, he exhibits them.

Thus it was half a century ago. I was contemporary with such men. I knew Orgaryev and Herzen themselves, and others of that stamp, and men educated in the same traditions. There was a remarkable absence of consistency in the lives of all these men. Together with a sincere and ardent wish for good there was an utter looseness of personal desire, which they thought could not hinder the living of a good life nor the performance of good and even great deeds.

They put unkneaded loaves into a cold oven and believed that bread would be baked. And then, when with advancing years they began to notice that the bread did not bake—i.e. that no good came of their lives—they saw in this something peculiarly tragic.

And the tragedy of such lives is indeed terrible. And this same tragedy apparent in the lives of Herzen, Ogaryev, and others of their time, exists today in the lives of very many so-called educated people who hold the same views.

A man desires to lead a good life, but the consecutiveness which is indispensable for this is lost in the society in which he lives. The majority of men of the present day, like Ogaryev, Herzen and others fifty years ago, are persuaded that to lead an effeminate life, to eat sweet and rich foods, to delight themselves in every way and satisfy all their desires, does not hinder them from living a good life. But as it is evident that a good life in their case does not result, they give themselves up to pessimism, and say, "Such is the tragedy of human life."

It is strange too that these people, who know that the distribution of pleasures among men is unequal and regard this inequality as an evil and wish to correct it, yet do not cease to strive to augment their own pleasures—that is, to augment inequality in the distribution of pleasures. In acting thus, these people are like men who being the first to enter an orchard hasten to gather all the fruit they can lay their hands on, and while professing a wish to organize a more equal distribution of the fruit of the orchard between themselves and later comers, continue to pluck all they can reach.

The delusion that men while addicting themselves to their desires and regarding this life of desire as good, can yet lead a good, useful, just, and loving life, is so astonishing that men of later generations will, I should think, simply fail to understand what the men of our time meant by the words "good life", when they said that the gluttons—the effeminate, lustful sluggards—of our wealthy classes led good lives.

Indeed, one need only put aside for a moment the customary view of the life of our wealthy classes, and look at it, I do not say from the Christian point of view, but from the pagan standpoint, from the standpoint of the very lowest demands of justice, to be convinced that, living amidst the violation of the plainest laws of justice or fairness, such as even children in their games think it wrong to violate, we men of the wealthy classes have no right even to talk about a good life.

Any man of our society who would, I do not say begin a good life but even begin to make some little approach towards it, must first of all cease to lead a bad life, must begin to destroy those conditions of an evil life with which he finds himself surrounded.

How often one hears, as an excuse for not reforming

our lives, the argument that any act that is contrary to the usual mode of life would be unnatural, ludicrous—would look like a desire to show off, and would therefore not be a good action. This argument seems expressly framed to prevent people from ever changing their lives.

If all our life were good, just, kind, then and only then would an action in conformity with the usual mode of life be good. If half our life were good and the other half bad, then there would be as much chance of an action not in conformity with the usual mode of life being good as of its being bad. But when life is altogether bad and wrong, as is the case of our upper classes, then a man cannot perform a single good action without disturbing the usual current of life. He can do a bad action without disturbing this current, but not a good one.

A man accustomed to the life of our well-to-do classes cannot lead a righteous life without first coming out of those conditions of evil in which he is immersed—he cannot begin to do good until he has ceased to do evil.

It is impossible for a man living in luxury to lead a righteous life. All his efforts after goodness will be in vain until he changes his life, until he performs that work which stands first in sequence before him. A good life according to the pagan view, and still more according to the Christian view, is, and can be, measured in no other way than by the mathematical relation between love of self and love of others. The less there is of love of self with all the ensuing care about self and the selfish demands made upon the labor of others, and the more there is of love of others with the resultant care for and labor bestowed upon others, the better is the life.

Thus has goodness of life been understood by all the sages of the world and by all true Christians, and in exactly the same way do all plain men understand it now. The more a man gives to others and the less he demands for himself, the better he is: the less he gives to others and the more he demands for himself, the worse he is.

And not only does a man become morally better the more love he has for others and the less for himself, but the less he loves himself the easier it becomes for him to be better, and contrariwise.

The more a man loves himself, and consequently the more he demands labor from others, the less possibility is there for him to love and to work for others; less not only by as much as the increase of his love for himself, but less in an enormously greater degree—just as when we move the fulcrum of a lever from the long end towards the short end, we not only increase the long arm but also reduce the short one. Therefore if a man possessing a certain faculty (love) augments his love and care for himself, he thereby diminishes his power of loving and caring for others not only in proportion to the love he has transferred to himself but in a much greater degree. Instead of feeding others a man eats too much himself; by so doing he not only diminishes the possibility of giving away the surplus, but by overeating deprives himself of power to help others.

In order to love others in reality and not in word only, one must cease to love oneself also in reality and not merely in word. In most cases it happens thus: we think we love others, we assure ourselves and others that it is so, but we love them only in words while we love ourselves in reality. We forget to feed and put others to bed, ourselves—never. Therefore, in order really to love others in deed, we must learn not to love ourselves in deed, learn to forget to feed ourselves and put ourselves to bed, exactly as we forget to do these things for others.

We say of a self-indulgent person accustomed to lead a luxurious life, that he is a "good man" and "leads a good life". But such a person—whether man or woman—although he may possess the most amiable traits of character, meekness, good nature, etc., cannot be good and lead a good life, any more than a knife of the very best workmanship and steel can be sharp and cut well unless it is sharpened.

To be good and lead a good life means to give to others more than one takes from them. But a self-indulgent man accustomed to a luxurious life cannot do this, first because he himself always needs a great deal (and this not because he is selfish, but because he is accustomed to luxury and finds it painful to be deprived of that to which he is accustomed); and secondly, because by consuming all that he receives from others he weakens himself and renders himself unfit for labor, and therefore unfit to serve others.

A self-indulgent man who sleeps long upon a soft bed and consumes an abundance of rich, sweet food, who always wears clean clothes and such as are suited to the temperature, who has never accustomed himself to the effort of laborious work, can do very little.

We are so accustomed to our own lies and the lies of others, and it is so convenient for us not to see through the lies of others that they may not see through ours, that we are not in the least astonished at, and do not doubt the truth of, the assertion of the virtue, sometimes even the sanctity, of people who are leading a perfectly unrestrained life.

A person, man or woman, sleeps on a spring bed with two mattresses, two smooth clean sheets, and feather pillows in pillow-cases. By the bedside is a rug that the feet may not get cold on stepping out of bed, though slippers also lie near. Here also are the necessary utensils so that he need not leave the house—whatever uncleanliness he may produce will be carried away and all made tidy. The windows are covered with curtains that the daylight may not awaken him, and he sleeps as long as he is inclined. Besides all this, measures are taken that the room may be warm in winter and cool in summer, and that he may not be disturbed by the noise of flies or other insects.

While he sleeps hot and cold water for his ablutions, and sometimes baths and preparations for shaving, are provided. Tea and coffee are also prepared, stimulating drinks to be taken immediately upon rising. Boots, shoes, galoshes—several pairs dirtied the previous day— are already being cleaned, freed from every speck of dust, and made to shine like glass.

Other various garments soiled on the preceding day are similarly cleaned, and these differ in texture to suit not only summer and winter, but also spring, autumn, rainy, damp, and warm weather. Clean linen, washed, starched, and ironed, is being made ready, with studs, shirt buttons, and buttonholes, all carefully inspected by specially appointed people.

If the person be active he rises early—at seven o'clock —but still a couple of hours later than those who are making all these preparations for him. And besides clothes for the day and covering for the night there is also a special costume and footgear for him while he is dressing—dressing-gown and slippers. And now he undertakes his washing, cleaning, brushing, for which several kinds of brushes are used as well as soap and a great quantity of water. (Many English men and women, for some reason or other, are specially proud of using a great deal of soap and pouring a large quantity of water over themselves.)

Then he dresses, brushes his hair before a special kind of looking-glass (different from those that hang in almost every room in the house), takes the things he needs, such as spectacles or eyeglasses, and then distributes in different pockets a clean pocket-handkerchief to blow his nose on; a watch with a chain, though in almost every room he goes to there will be a clock; money of various kinds, small change (often in a specially contrived case which saves him the trouble of looking for the required coin) and bank-notes; also visiting cards on which his name is printed (saving him the trouble of saying or writing it); pocket-book and pencil.

In the case of women, the toilet is still more complicated: corsets, arranging of long hair, adornments, laces, elastics, ribbons, ties, hairpins, pins, brooches.

But at last all is complete and the day commences, generally with eating: tea and coffee are drunk with a great quantity of sugar; bread made of the finest white flour is eaten with large quantities of butter, and sometimes the flesh of pigs.

The men for the most part smoke cigars or cigarettes meanwhile, and read fresh papers which have just been brought. Then, leaving to others the task of setting right the soiled and disordered room, they go to their office or business, or drive in carriages produced specially to move such people about.

Then comes a luncheon of slain beasts, birds, and fish, followed by a dinner consisting, if it be very modest, of three courses, dessert, and coffee. Then playing at cards and playing music—or the theater, reading, and conversation in soft spring armchairs by the intensified and shaded light of candles, gas, or electricity. After this, more tea, more eating—supper—and to bed again, the bed shaken up and prepared with clean linen, and the utensils washed to be made foul again.

Thus pass the days of a man of modest life, of whom, if he is good-natured and does not possess any habits specially obnoxious to those about him, it is said that he leads a good and virtuous life.

But a good life is the life of a man who does good to others; and can a man accustomed to live thus do good to others? Before he can do good to men he must cease to do evil. Reckon up all the harm such a man, often unconsciously, does to others, and you will see that he is far indeed from doing good. He would have to perform many acts of heroism to redeem the evil he commits, but he is too much enfeebled by his self-created needs to perform any such acts.

He might sleep with more advantage, both physical and moral, lying on the floor wrapped in his cloak as Marcus Aurelius did; thus saving all the labor and trouble involved in the manufacture of mattresses, springs, and pillows, as well as the daily labor of the laundress—one of the weaker sex burdened by the bearing and nursing of children—who washes linen for this strong man.

By going to bed earlier and getting up earlier he might save window-curtains and the evening lamp.

He might sleep in the same shirt he wears during the day, might step barefooted upon the floor, and go out into the yard; he might wash at the pump.

In a word, he might live like those who work for him, and thus save all this work that is done for him. He might save all the labor expended upon his clothing, his refined food, his recreations. And he knows under what conditions all these labors are performed: how men perish and suffer in performing them, and how they often hate those who take advantage of their poverty to force them to do it.

How then can such a man do good to others and lead a righteous life, without abandoning this self-indulgence and luxury?

But we need not speak of how other people appear in our eyes—everyone must see and feel this concerning himself.

I cannot but repeat this same thing again and again, notwithstanding the cold and hostile silence with which my words are recieved. A moral man, living a life of comfort, a man even of the middle class (I will not speak of the upper classes, who daily consume the results of hundreds of working days to satisfy their caprices), cannot live quietly, knowing that all he is using is produced by the labor of working people whose lives are crushed, who are dying without hope—ignorant, drunken, dissolute, semi-savage creatures employed in mines, factories, and in agricultural labor, producing the things that he uses.

At the present moment I who am writing this and you who will read it, whoever you may be—have wholesome, sufficient, perhaps abundant and luxurious food, pure warm air to breathe, winter and summer clothing, various recreations, and, most important of all, leisure by day and undisturbed repose at night.

And here by our side live the working people, who have neither wholesome food nor healthy lodgings nor sufficient clothing nor recreations, and who above all are deprived not only of leisure but even of rest: old men, children, women, worn out by labor, by sleepless nights, by disease, who spend their whole lives providing for us those articles of comfort and luxury which they do not possess, and which are for us not necessities but super-fluities.

Therefore a moral man (I do not say a Christian, but simply a man professing humane views or merely esteeming justice) cannot but wish to change his life and to cease to use articles of luxury produced under such conditions.

If a man really pities those who manufacture tobacco, then the first thing he will naturally do will be to cease smoking, because by continuing to buy and smoke tobacco he encourages the preparation of tobacco by which men's health is destroyed. And so with every other article of luxury. If a man can still continue to eat bread notwithstanding the hard work by which it is produced, this is because he cannot forgo what is indispensable while waiting for the present conditions of labor to be altered. But with regard to things which are not only unnecessary but are even superfluous there can be no other conclusion than this: that if I pity men engaged in the manufacture of certain articles, then I must on no account accustom myself to require such articles.

But nowadays men argue otherwise. They invent the most varied and intricate arguments, but never say what naturally occurs to every plain man. According to them, it is not at all necessary to abstain from luxuries. One can sympathize with the condition of the working men, deliver speeches and write books on their behalf, and at the same time continue to profit by the labor that one sees to be ruinous to them.

According to one argument, I may profit by labor that is harmful to the workers because if I do not another will.

Which is something like the argument that I must drink wine that is injurious to me because it has been bought and if I do not drink it others will.

According to another argument, it is even beneficial to the workers to be allowed to produce luxuries, for in this way we provide them with money—that is, with the means of subsistence: as if we could not provide them with the means of subsistence in any other way than by making them produce articles injurious to them and superfluous to us.

But according to a third argument, now most popular, it seems that, since there is such a thing as division of labor, any work upon which a man is engaged—whether he be a Government official, priest, landowner, manufacturer, or merchant—is so useful that it fully compensates for the labor of the working classes by which he profits.

One serves the State, another the Church, a third science, a fourth art, and a fifth serves those who serve the State, science, and art; and all are firmly convinced that what they give to mankind certainly compensates for all they take. And it is astonishing how, while continually augmenting their luxurious requirements without increasing their activity, these people continue to be certain that their activity compensates for all they consume.

Whereas if you listen to these people's judgement of one another it appears that each individual is far from being worth what he consumes. Government officials say that the work of the landlords is not worth what they spend, landlords say the same about merchants, and merchants about Government officials, and so on. But this does not disconcert them, and they continue to assure people that they (each of them) profit by the labors of others exactly in proportion to the service they render to others. So that the payment is not determined by the work, but the value of the imaginary work is determined by the payment.

Thus they assure one another, but they know perfectly well in the depth of their souls that all their arguments do not justify them; that they are not necessary to the working men, and that they profit by the labor of those men not on account of any division of labor but simply because they have the power to do so, and because they are so spoiled that they cannot do without it.

And all this arises from people imagining that it is possible to lead a good life without first acquiring the primary quality necessary for a good life.

And that first quality is self-control.

There never has been and cannot be a good life without self-control. Apart from self-control no good life is imaginable. The attainment of goodness must begin with that.

There is a scale of virtues, and if one would mount the higher steps it is necessary to begin with the lowest; and the first virtue a man must acquire if he wishes to acquire the others is that which the ancients called ἐγκράτεια or σωφροσύνη—that is, self-control or moderation.

If in the Christian teaching self-control was included in the conception of self-renunciation, still the order of succession remained the same, and the acquirement of any Christian virtue is impossible without self-control—and this not because such a rule has been invented, but because it is the essential nature of the case.

But even self-control, the first step in every righteous life, is not attainable all at once but only by degrees.

Self-control is the liberation of man from desires—their subordination to moderation, σωφροσύνη. But a man's desires are many and various, and in order to contend with them successfully he must begin with the fundamental ones—those upon which the more complex

ones have grown up—and not with those complex lusts which have grown up upon the fundamental ones. There are complex lusts like that of the adornment of the body, sports, amusements, idle talk, inquisitiveness, and many others; and there are also fundamental lusts—gluttony, idleness, sexual love.

And one must begin to contend with these lusts from the beginning; not with the complex but with the fundamental ones, and that also in a definite order. And this order is determined both by the nature of things and by the tradition of human wisdom.

A man who eats too much cannot strive against laziness, while a gluttonous and idle man will never be able to contend with sexual lust. Therefore, according to all moral teachings, the effort towards self-control commenses with a struggle against the lust of gluttony—commences with fasting. In our time, however, every serious relation to the attainment of a good life has been so long and so completely lost that not only is the very first virtue —self-control—without which the others are unattainable, regarded as superfluous, but the order of succession necessary for the attainment of this first virtue is also disregarded, and fasting is quite forgotten, or is looked upon as a silly superstition, utterly unnecessary.

And yet, just as the first condition of a good life is self-control, so the first condition of a life of self-control is fasting.

One may wish to be good, one may dream of goodness, without fasting; but to *be* good without fasting is as impossible as it is to advance without getting up on one's feet.

Fasting is an indispensable condition of a good life, whereas gluttony is and always has been the first sign of the opposite; and unfortunately this vice is in the highest degree characteristic of the life of the majority of the men of our time.

Look at the faces and figures of the men of our circle and day. On all those faces with pendent cheeks and chins, those corpulent limbs and prominent stomachs, lies the indelible seal of a dissolute life. Nor can it be otherwise. Consider our life and the actuating motive of the majority of men in our society, and then ask yourself, What is the chief interest of this majority? And, strange as it may appear to us who are accustomed to hide our real interests and to profess false, artificial ones, you will find that the chief interest of their life is the satisfaction of the palate, the pleasure of eating—gluttony.

From the poorest to the richest, eating is, I think, the chief aim, the chief pleasure, of our life. Poor working people form an exception, but only inasmuch as want prevents their addicting themselves to this passion. No sooner have they the time and the means, than, in imitation of the higher classes, they procure rich and tasty foods, and eat and drink as much as they can. The more they eat the more do they deem themselves not only happy, but also strong and healthy. And in this conviction they are encouraged by the upper classes, who regard food in precisely the same way.

The educated classes (following the medical men who assure them that the most expensive food, flesh, is the most wholesome), imagine that happiness and health consist in tasty, nourishing, easily digested food—in gorging—though they try to conceal this.

Look at rich people's lives, listen to their conversation. What lofty subjects seem to occupy them: philosophy, science, art, poetry, the distribution of wealth, the welfare of the people, and the education of the young! But all this is, for the immense majority, a sham. All this occupies them only in the intervals of business, real business: in the intervals, that is, between lunch and

dinner, while the stomach is full and it is impossible to eat more. The only real living interest of the majority both of men and women, especially after early youth, is eating—How to eat, what to eat, where to eat, and when to eat.

No solemnity, no rejoicing, no consecration, no opening of anything, can dispense with eating.

Watch people travelling. In their case the thing is specially evident. "Museums, libraries, Parliament—how very interesting! But where shall we dine? Where is one best fed?" Look at people when they come together for dinner, dressed up, perfumed, around a table decorated with flowers—how joyfully they rub their hands and smile!

If we could look into the hearts of the majority of people what should we find they most desire? Appetite for breakfast and for dinner. What is the severest punishment from infancy upwards? To be put on bread and water. What artisans get the highest wages? Cooks. What is the chief interest of the mistress of the house? To what subject does the conversation of middle-class housewives generally tend?

If the conversation of the members of the higher classes does not tend in the same direction it is not because they are better educated or are occupied with higher interests, but simply because they have a housekeeper or a steward who relieves them of all anxiety about their dinner. But once deprive them of this convenience and you will see what causes them most anxiety. It all comes round to the subject of eating: the price of grouse, the best way of making coffee, of baking sweet cakes, and so on.

People come together whatever the occasion—a christening, a funeral, a wedding, the consecration of a church, the departure or arrival of a friend, the consecration of regimental colors, the celebration of a memorable day, the death or birth of a great scientist, philosopher, or teacher of morality—men come together as if occupied by the most lofty interests. But it is only a pretense: they all know that there will be eating—good tasty food—and drinking, and it is chiefly this that brings them together.

To this end, for several days before, animals have been slaughtered, baskets of provisions brought from gastronomic shops, cooks and their helpers, kitchen boys and maids, specially attired in clean, starched frocks and caps, have been "at work". Chefs, receiving £50 a month and more, have been occupied in giving directions. Cooks have been chopping, kneading, roasting, arranging, adorning. With like solemnity and importance a master of the ceremonies has been working, calculating, pondering, adjusting, with his eye, like an artist. A gardener has been employed upon the flowers. Scullerymaids. . . .

An army of men has been at work, the result of thousands of working days are being swallowed up, and all this that people may come together to talk about some great teacher of science or morality, or recall the memory of a deceased friend, or to greet a young couple just entering upon a new life.

In the middle and lower classes it is perfectly evident that every festivity, every funeral or wedding, means gluttony. There the matter is so understood. To such an extent is gluttony the motive of the assembly that in Greek and in French the same word means both *wedding* and *feast*.

But in the upper classes of the rich, especially among the refined who have long possessed wealth, great skill is used to conceal this and to make it appear that eating is a secondary matter necessary only for appearance. And this pretence is easy, for in the majority of cases the guests are satiated in the true sense of the word—they are never hungry.

They pretend that dinner, eating, is not necessary to them, is even a burden; but this is a lie. Try giving them —instead of the refined dishes they expect—I do not say bread and water, but porridge or gruel or something of that kind, and see what a storm it will call forth and how evident will become the real truth, namely, that the chief interest of the assembly is not the ostensible one but— gluttony.

Look at what men sell. Go through a town and see what men buy—articles of adornment and things to devour.

And indeed this must be so, it cannot be otherwise. It is only possible not to think about eating, to keep this lust under control, when a man does not eat except in obedience to necessity. If a man *ceases* to eat only in obedience to necessity—if, that is, he eats when the stomach is full—then the state of things cannot but be what it actually is.

If men love the pleasure of eating, if they allow themselves to love this pleasure, if they find it good (as in the case with the vast majority of men in our time, and with educated men quite as much as with uneducated, though they pretend that it is not so), there is no limit to the augmentation of this pleasure, no limit beyond which it may not grow. The satisfaction of a *need* has limits, but pleasure has none. For the satisfaction of our needs it is necessary and sufficient to eat bread, porridge, or rice; for the augmentation of a pleasure there is no end to the possible flavorings and seasonings.

Bread is a necessary and sufficient food. (This is proved by the millions of men who are strong, active, healthy, and hard-working on rye bread alone.) But it is pleasanter to eat bread with some flavoring. It is well to soak the bread in water boiled with meat. Still better to put into this water some vegetable or, even better, several vegetables.

It is well to eat flesh. And flesh is better not stewed, but roasted. It is better still with butter, and underdone, and choosing out certain special parts of the meat. But add to this vegetables and mustard. And drink wine with it, red wine for preference.

One does not need any more, but one can still eat some fish if it is well flavored with sauces and swallowed down with white wine. It would seem as if one could get through nothing more, either rich or tasty, but a sweet dish can still be managed; in summer ices, in winter stewed fruits, preserves, and the like.

And thus we have a dinner, a modest dinner. The pleasure of such a dinner can be greatly augmented. And it is augmented, and there is no limit to this augmentation: stimulating snacks, *hors-d'oeuvres* before dinner, and *entremets* and desserts, and various combinations of tasty things, and flowers and decorations and music during dinner.

And strange to say, men who daily overeat themselves at such dinners—in comparison with which the feast of Belshazzar that evoked the prophetic warning was nothing—are naively persuaded that they may yet be leading a moral life.

Fasting is an indispensable condition of a good life; but in fasting, as in self-control in general, the question arises, what shall we begin with?—How to fast, how often to eat, what to eat, what to avoid eating? And as we can do no work seriously without regarding the necessary order of sequence, so also we cannot fast without knowing where to begin—with what to commence self-control in food.

Fasting! And even an analysis of how to fast and where to begin! The notion seems ridiculous and wild to the majority of men.

I remember how an Evangelical preacher who was attacking monastic asceticism once said to me with pride at his own originality, "Ours is not a Christianity of fasting and privations, but of beefsteaks." Christianity, or virtue in general—and beefsteaks!

During a long period of darkness and lack of all guidance, Pagan or Christian, so many wild, immoral ideas have made their way into our life (especially into that lower region of the first steps towards a good life—our relation to food to which no one paid any attention), that it is difficult for us in our days even to understand the audacity and senselessness of upholding Christianity or virtue with beefsteaks.

We are not horrified by this association simply because a strange thing has befallen us. We look and see not; listen and hear not. There is no bad odor, no sound, no monstrosity, to which man cannot become so accustomed that he ceases to remark what would strike a man unaccustomed to it. And it is precisely the same in the moral region. Christianity and morality with beefsteaks!

A few days ago I visited the slaughter-house in our town of Tula. It is built on the new and improved system practiced in large towns, with a view to causing the animals as little suffering as possible. It was on a Friday, two days before Trinity Sunday. There were many cattle there.

Long before this, when reading that excellent book, *The Ethics of Diet*, I had wished to visit a slaughter-house in order to see with my own eyes the reality of the question raised when vegetarianism is discussed. But at first I felt ashamed to do so, as one is always ashamed of going to look at suffering which one knows is about to take place but which one cannot avert; and so I kept putting off my visit.

But a little while ago I met on the road a butcher returning to Tula after a visit to his home. He is not yet an experienced butcher, and his duty is to stab with a knife. I asked him whether he did not feel sorry for the animals that he killed. He gave me the usual answer: "Why should I feel sorry? It is necessary." But when I told him that eating flesh is not necessary, but is only a luxury, he agreed; and then he admitted that he was sorry for the animals.

"But what can I do?" he said, "I must earn my bread. At first I was *afraid* to kill. My father, he never even killed a chicken in all his life."

The majority of Russians cannot kill; they feel pity, and express the feeling by the word *fear*. This man had also been "afraid," but he was so no longer. He told me that most of the work was done on Fridays, when it continues until the evening.

Not long ago I also had a talk with a retired soldier, a butcher, and he too was surprised at my assertion that it was a pity to kill, and said the usual things about its being ordained. But afterwards he agreed with me: "Especially when they are quiet, tame cattle. They come, poor things! trusting you. It is very pitiful."

This is dreadful! Not the suffering and death of the animals, but that man suppresses in himself, unnecessarily, the highest spiritual capacity—that of sympathy and pity towards living creatures like himself—and by violating his own feelings becomes cruel. And how deeply seated in the human heart is the injunction not to take life!

Once, when walking from Moscow,* I was offered a

---

* When returning to Yasnaya Polyana in spring after his winter's resi-
dence in Moscow, Tolstoy repeatedly chose to walk the distance

lift by some carters who were going from Serpukhov to a neighboring forest to fetch wood. It was the Thursday before Easter. I was seated in the first cart with a strong, red, coarse carman, who evidently drank. On entering a village we saw a well-fed, naked, pink pig being dragged out of the first yard to be slaughtered. It squealed in a dreadful voice, resembling the shriek of a man. Just as we were passing they began to kill it.

A man gashed its throat with a knife. The pig squealed still more loudly and piercingly, broke away from the men, and ran off covered with blood. Being near-sighted I did not see all the details. I saw only the human-looking pink body of the pig and heard its desperate squeal, but the carter saw all the details and watched closely. They caught the pig, knocked it down, and finished cutting its throat. When its squeals ceased the carter sighed heavily. "Do men really not have to answer for such things?" he said.

So strong is man's aversion to all killing. But by example, by encouraging greediness, by the assertion that God has allowed it, and above all by habit, people entirely lose this natural feeling.

On Friday I decided to go to Tula, and, meeting a meek, kind acquaintance of mine, I invited him to accompany me.

"Yes, I have heard that the arrangements are good, and have been wishing to go and see it; but if they are slaughtering I will not go in."

"Why not? That's just what I want to see! If we eat flesh it must be killed."

"No, no, I cannot!"

It is worth remarking that this man is a sportsman and

(something over 130 miles) instead of going by rail. Serpukhov is a town he had to pass on the way.

himself kills animals and birds.

So we went to the slaughter-house. Even at the entrance one noticed the heavy, disgusting, fetid smell, as of carpenter's glue, or paint on glue. The nearer we approached the stronger became the smell. The building is of red brick, very large, with vaults and high chimneys. We entered the gates.

To the right was a spacious enclosed yard, three-quarters of an acre in extent—twice a week cattle are driven in here for sale—and adjoining this enclosure was the porter's lodge. To the left were the chambers, as they are called—i.e. rooms with arched entrances, sloping asphalt floors, and contrivances for moving and hanging up the carcasses.

On a bench against the wall of the porter's lodge were seated half a dozen butchers, in aprons covered with blood, their tucked-up sleeves disclosing their muscular arms also besmeared with blood. They had finished their work half an hour before, so that day we could only see the empty chambers. Though these chambers were open on both sides, there was an oppressive smell of warm blood; the floor was brown and shining, with congealed black blood in the cavities.

One of the butchers described the process of slaughtering, and showed us the place where it was done. I did not quite understand him, and formed a wrong, but very horrible, idea of the way the animals are slaughtered; and I fancied that, as is often the case the reality would very likely produce upon me a weaker impression than the imagination. But in this I was mistaken.

The next time I visited the slaughter-house I went in good time. It was the Friday before Trinity—a warm day in June. The smell of glue and blood was even stronger and more penetrating than on my first visit. The work was at its height. The dusty yard was full of cattle, and animals had been driven into all the enclosures beside the chambers.

In the street before the entrance stood carts to which oxen, calves, and cows were tied. Other carts drawn by good horses and filled with live calves, whose heads hung down and swayed about, drew up and were unloaded; and similar carts containing the carcasses of oxen, with trembling legs sticking out, with heads and bright red lungs and brown livers, drove away from the slaughter-house.

By the fence stood the cattle-dealers' horses. The dealers themselves, in their long coats, with their whips and knouts in their hands, were walking about the yard, either marking with tar cattle belonging to the same owner, or bargaining, or else guiding oxen and bulls from the great yard into the enclosures which lead into the chambers. These men were evidently all preoccupied with money matters and calculations, and any thought as to whether it was right or wrong to kill these animals was as far from their minds as were questions about the chemical composition of the blood that covered the floor of the chambers.

No butchers were to be seen in the yard; they were all in the chambers at work. That day about a hundred head of cattle were slaughtered. I was on the point of entering one of the chambers, but stopped short at the door. I stopped both because the chamber was crowded with carcasses which were being moved about, and also because blood was flowing on the floor and dripping from above. All the butchers present were besmeared with blood, and had I entered I, too, should certainly have been covered with it. One suspended carcass was being taken down, another was being moved towards the door, a third, a slaughtered ox, was lying with its white legs raised, while a butcher with strong hand was ripping up its tight-stretched hide.

Through the door opposite the one at which I was standing, a big, red, well-fed ox was led in. Two men were dragging it, and hardly had it entered when I saw a butcher raise a knife above its neck and stab it. The ox, as if all four legs had suddenly given way, fell heavily on its belly, immediately turned over on one side, and began to work its legs and its whole hind-quarters.

Another butcher at once threw himself upon the ox from the side opposite to the twitching legs, caught its horns and twisted its head down to the ground, while another butcher cut its throat with a knife. From beneath the head there flowed a stream of blackish-red blood, which a besmeared boy caught in a tin basin. All the time this was going on the ox kept incessantly twitching its head as if trying to get up, and waved its four legs in the air.

The basin was quickly filling, but the ox still lived, and, its stomach heaving heavily, both hind and fore legs worked so violently that the butchers held aloof. When one basin was full the boy carried it away on his head to the albumen factory, while another boy placed a fresh basin, which also soon began to fill up. But still the ox heaved its body and worked its hind legs.

When the blood ceased to flow the butcher raised the animal's head and began to skin it. The ox continued to writhe. The head, stripped of its skin, showed red with white veins, and kept the position given it by the butcher; the skin hung on both sides. Still the animal did not cease to writhe. Then another butcher caught hold of one of the legs, broke it, and cut it off. In the remaining legs and the stomach the convulsions still continued. The other legs were cut off and thrown aside, together with those of other oxen belonging to the same owner. Then the carcass was dragged to the hoist and hung up and the

convulsions were over.

Thus I looked on from the door at the second, third, and fourth ox. It was the same with each: the same cutting off of the head with bitten tongue, and the same same convulsive members. The only difference was that the butcher did not always strike at once so as to cause the animal's fall. Sometimes he missed his aim, whereupon the ox tried to escape. But then his head was pulled under a bar, struck a second time, and he fell.

I afterwards entered by the door at which the oxen were led in. Here I saw the same thing, only nearer, and therefore more plainly. But chiefly I saw here, what I had not seen before, how the oxen were forced to enter this door. Each time an ox was seized in the enclosure and pulled forward by a rope tied to its horns, the animal, smelling blood, refused to advance, and sometimes bellowed and drew back. It would have been beyond the strength of two men to drag it in by force, so one of the butchers went round each time, grasped the animal's tail, and twisted it so violently that the gristle crackled, and the ox advanced.

When they had finished with the cattle of one owner they brought in those of another. The first animal of this next lot was not an ox but a bull—a fine, well-bred creature, black, with white spots on its legs, young, muscular, full of energy. He was dragged forward, but he lowered his head and resisted sturdily. Then the butcher who followed behind seized the tail like an engine-driver grasping the handle of a whistle, twisted it, the gristle crackled, and the bull rushed forward, upsetting the men who held the rope. Then it stopped, looking sideways with its black eyes, the whites of which had filled with blood. But again the tail crackled, and the bull sprang forward and reached the required spot.

The striker approached, took aim, and struck. But the

blow missed the mark. The bull leaped up, shook his head, bellowed, and, covered with blood, broke free and rushed back. The men at the doorway all sprang aside; but the experienced butchers, with the dash of men inured to danger, quickly caught the rope; again the tail operation was repeated, and again the bull was in the chamber, where he was dragged under the bar, from which he did not again escape. The striker quickly took aim at the spot where the hair divides like a star, and, notwithstanding the blood, found it, struck, and the fine animal, full of life, collapsed, its head and legs writhing while it was bled and the head skinned.

"There, the cursed devil hasn't even fallen the right way!" grumbled the butcher as he cut the skin from the head.

Five minutes later the head was stuck up, red instead of black, without skin; the eyes that had shone with such splendid color five minutes before, fixed and glassy.

Afterwards I went into the compartment where small animals are slaughtered—a very large chamber with asphalt floor, and tables with backs, on which sheep and calves are killed. Here the work was already finished; in the long room, impregnated with the smell of blood, were only two butchers. One was blowing into the leg of a dead lamb and patting the swollen stomach with his hand; the other, a young fellow in an apron besmeared with blood, was smoking a bent cigarette. There was no one else in the long dark chamber, filled with a heavy smell.

After me there entered a man, apparently an ex-soldier, bringing in a young yearling ram, black with a white mark on its neck, and its legs tied. This animal he placed upon one of the tables as if upon a bed. The old soldier greeted the butchers, with whom he was evidently acquainted, and began to ask when their master allowed them leave. The fellow with the cigarette approached with a knife, sharpened it on the edge of the table, and answered that they were free on holidays. The live ram was lying as quietly as the dead inflated one, except that it was briskly wagging its short little tail and its sides were heaving more quickly than usual.

The soldier pressed down its uplifted head gently, without effort; the butcher, still continuing the conversation, grasped with his left hand the head of the ram and cut its throat. The ram quivered, and the little tail stiffened and ceased to wave. The fellow, while waiting for the blood to flow, began to relight his cigarette which had gone out. The blood flowed and the ram began to writhe. The conversation continued without the slightest interruption. It was horribly revolting.

And how about those hens and chickens which daily in thousands of kitchens, with heads cut off and streaming with blood, comically, dreadfully, flop about, jerking their wings?

And see, a kind, refined lady will devour the carcasses of these animals with full assurance that she is doing right, at the same time asserting two contradictory propositions:

First, that she is, as her doctor assures her, so delicate that she cannot be sustained by vegetable food alone and that for her feeble organism flesh is indispensable; and secondly, that she is so sensitive that she is unable, not only herself to inflict suffering on animals, but even to bear the sight of suffering.

Whereas the poor lady is weak precisely because she has been taught to live upon food unnatural to man; and she cannot avoid causing suffering to animals—for she eats them.

We cannot pretend that we do not know this. We are not ostriches, and cannot believe that if we refuse to look at what we do not wish to see, it will not exist. This is especially the case when what we do not wish to see is what we wish to eat. If it were really indispensable, or if not indispensable, at least in some way useful!

But it is quite unnecessary,* and only serves to develop animal feelings, to excite desire, and to promote fornication and drunkenness. And this is continually being confirmed by the fact that young, kind, undepraved people—especially women and girls—without knowing how it logically follows, feel that virtue is incompatible with beefsteaks, and, as soon as they wish to be good, give up eating flesh.

What, then, do I wish to say? That in order to be moral people must cease to eat meat? Not at all.

I only wish to say that for a good life a certain order of good actions is indispensable; that if a man's aspirations towards right living be serious they will inevitably follow one definite sequence; and that in this sequence the first virtue a man will strive after will be self-control, self-restraint. And in seeking for self-control a man will inevitably follow one definite sequence, and in this sequence the first thing will be self-control in food—fasting.

And in fasting, if he be really and seriously seeking to live a good life, the first thing from which he will abstain will always be the use of animal food, because, to say nothing of the excitation of the passions caused by such food, its use is simply immoral, as it involves the per-

---

* Let those who doubt this read the numerous books upon the subject, written by scientists and doctors, in which it is proved that flesh is not necessary for the nourishment of man. And let them not listen to those old-fashioned doctors who defend the assertion that flesh is necessary, merely because it has long been so regarded by their predecessors and by themselves; and who defend their opinion with tenacity and malevolence, as all that is old and traditional always is defended.

formance of an act which is contrary to moral feeling—
killing; and is called forth only by greediness and the desire for tasty food.

The precise reason why abstinence from animal food
will be the first act of fasting and of a moral life is ad-
mirably explained in the book, *The Ethics of Diet*; and
not by one man only, but by all mankind in the persons
of its best representatives during all the conscious life of
humanity.

But why, if the wrongfulness—i.e. the immorality—of
animal food was known to humanity so long ago, have
people not yet come to acknowledge this law? will be
asked by those who are accustomed to be led by public
opinion rather than by reason.

The answer to this question is that the moral progress
of humanity—which is the foundation of every other kind
of progress—is always slow; but that the sign of true, not
casual, progress is its uninterruptedness and its continu-
al acceleration.

And the progress of vegetarianism is of this kind. That
progress is expressed both in words of the writers cited in
the above-mentioned book and in the actual life of mankind, which from many causes is involuntarily passing
more and more from carnivorous habits to vegetable
food, and is also deliberately following the same path in a
movement which shows evident strength, and which is
growing larger and larger—viz. vegetarianism. That
movement has during the last ten years advanced more
and more rapidly. More and more books and periodicals
on this subject appear every year; one meets more and
more people who have given up meat; and abroad, especially in Germany, England, and America, the number
of vegetarian hotels and restaurants increases year by
year.

This movement should cause especial joy to those

whose life lies in the effort to bring about the kingdom of God on earth, not because vegetarianism is in itself an important step towards that kingdom (all true steps are both important and unimportant), but because it is a sign that the aspiration of mankind towards moral perfection is serious and sincere, for it has taken the one unalterable order of succession natural to it, beginning with the first step.

One cannot fail to rejoice at this, as people could not fail to rejoice, who, after striving to reach the upper story of a house by trying vainly and at random to climb the walls from different points, should at last assemble at the first step of the staircase and crowd towards it, convinced that there can be no way up except by mounting this first step of the stairs.

INDUSTRY AND IDLENESS

In the sweat of thy face shalt thou eat bread, till thou return unto the ground; for out of it wast thou taken.   *Gen. 3:19.*

The above are the title and the epigraph of a book by Timothy Mihaylovitch Bondaref* which I have read in manuscript.

That book seems to me very remarkable for its strength, its clearness, and the beauty of its language, as well as for a sincerity of conviction that is apparent in every line, but above all for the importance, truth, and depth of its fundamental thought.

The fundamental thought of the book is the following: In all the affairs of life the important thing is to know, not what is good and necessary, but what of all the good and necessary things in existence comes first in importance, what second, what third, and so on.

If that is important in worldly affairs, yet more is it important in matters of faith, which define man's duties.

* T.M. Bondaref was born a serf in 1820. In 1858 he was sent to serve for twenty-five years in the army, but joining the sect of "Sabbatari-

Tatian, a teacher of the early Church, says that men's sufferings come not so much from their not knowing God, as from their acknowledging a false god and esteeming as God that which is not God. The same thought applies to the duties men acknowledge. Misfortune and evil come, not so much from men not knowing their duties, as from the fact that they acknowledge false duties and esteem as duties things that are not really such, while they do not recognize as a duty that which is really their first duty.

Bondaref declares that the misfortunes and evil in men's lives come from regarding many empty and harmful regulations as religious duties, while forgetting, and hiding from themselves and others, that chief, primary, undoubted duty announced at the beginning of the Holy Scriptures: "In the sweat of thy face shalt thou eat bread."

For those who believe in the sanctity and infallibility of the word of God as expressed in the Bible, the command there given by God Himself, and nowhere revoked, is sufficient proof of its own validity. But for those who do not acknowledge the Holy Scriptures, the importance and validity of this commandment (if only it be considered without prejudice as a simple, not supernatural, expression of human wisdom) may be proved by a consideration of the conditions of human life, as is done by Bondaref in his book.

An obstacle to such consideration unfortunately exists

---

ans" (who accept the Old Testament as authoritative, and follow the Jewish faith in many things), he was banished in 1867 to Udina in Siberia. There, as a plowman of great energy, he built up for himself a fairly comfortable peasant home, but again impoverished himself by efforts to spread his doctrine of "bread-labor." His book could not be published in Russia, but has been translated into French and other languages. Another title Bondaref gave to his book is *The Agriculturist's Triumph*.

in the fact that many of us are so accustomed to hear from theologians perverted and senseless interpretations of the words of Holy Scripture, that the mere reminder that a certain principle coincides with the teachings of Scripture, is enough to cause some people to distrust that principle.

"What do I care for the Holy Scriptures? We know that anything you like can be deduced from them, and that they are all rubbish."

But this is unreasonable. Surely the Holy Scriptures are not to blame because people interpret them falsely; and a man who says what is true, is not to blame because the truth he utters is contained in the Holy Scriptures.

One must not forget that, if it be granted that what are called the Scriptures are human productions, it has still to be explained why just these human writings, and not some others, have come to be regarded by men as the words of God Himself. There must be some reason for it.

And the reason is clear.

Superstitious people called the Scriptures Divine because they were superior to anything else that people knew; and that is also the reason why these Scriptures, though always rejected by some men, have survived and are still considered Divine. These Scriptures are called Divine and have come down to us because they contain the highest human wisdom. And, in many of its parts, such is really the character of the Scriptures called the Bible.

And such, among these Scriptures, is that forgotten, neglected, and misunderstood saying which Bondaref has explained and set at the head of the corner.

That saying, and the whole story of Paradise, are commonly taken in a literal sense, as though everything actually happened as described; whereas the meaning of the whole narrative is, that it figuratively represents the

conflicting tendencies which exist in human nature.

Man fears death, but is subject to it. Man seems happier while ignorant of good and evil, yet strives irresistibly to reach that knowledge. Man loves idleness, and wishes to satisfy his desires without suffering, yet only by labor and suffering can he or his race have life.

The sentence Bondaref quotes is important, not because it is supposed to have been said by God to Adam, but because it is true; it states one of the indubitable laws of human life. The law of gravity is not true because it was stated by Newton; but I know of Newton, and am grateful to him, because he showed an eternal law which explains to me a whole series of facts.

It is the same with the law: "In the sweat of thy face shalt thou eat bread." That is a law which explains to me a whole series of facts. And having once known it, I cannot forget it, and am grateful to him who revealed it to me.

This law seems very simple and familiar, but that is only apparently so; and to convince one's self of that fact we need only look around us. Not only do people not acknowledge this law, but they acknowledge the very reverse of it. People's belief leads them (from king to beggar) to strive, not to fulfil that law but to avoid fulfilling it. Bondaref's book is devoted to explaining the permanence and immutability of that law, and the inevitable sufferings that flow from its neglect.

Bondaref calls that law the "first-born" and chief of all laws.

Bondaref demonstrates that sins—*i.e.*, mistakes, false actions—result solely from the violation of this law. Of all the definite duties of man, Bondaref considers that the chief, primary, and most immutable for every man, is to earn his bread with his own hands, understanding by bread-labor all heavy rough work necessary to save man from death by hunger and cold, and by "bread" food, drink, clothes, shelter, and fuel.

Bondaref's fundamental thought is that this law—that to live man must work—heretofore acknowledge as inevitable, should be acknowledged as being a beneficent law of life, obligatory on everyone.

This law should be acknowledged as a religious law, like keeping the Sabbath or being circumcised among the Jews, like receiving the Sacrament or fasting among church Christians, like praying five times a day among the Mohammedans. Bondaref says, in one place, that if people but recognized bread-labor as a religious obligation, no private or special occupations could prevent their doing it, any more than special occupations prevent church people from keeping their holidays. There are about eighty holidays in the year,* but to perform "bread-labor," according to Bondaref's calculation, only forty days are needed.

However strange it may seem at first that such a simple method, intelligible to everyone, and involving nothing cunning or profound, can save humanity from its innumerable ills, yet more strange, when one comes to think of it, must it seem that we, having at hand so clear, simple, and long familiar a method, can, while neglecting it, seek a cure for our ills in various subtleties and profundities. Yet consider the matter well and you will see that such is the case.

A man omitting to fix a bottom to his tub, and then

---

* Saints' days are numerous in Russia, but on the other hand, no Saturday or other weekly half-holiday is customary, so that the total time allowed for holidays comes to much the same in Russia as in this country.

devising all sorts of cunning means to keep the water from running away, would typify all our efforts to heal existing ills.

Indeed, from what do all the ills of life arise, if we except those that people cause to one another directly, by murders, executions, imprisonments, fights, and the many cruelties in which men sin by using violence?

All the ills of humanity—except those produced by direct violence—come from hunger, from want of all kinds, from being overworked, or, on the other hand, from excess and idleness, and the vices they produce. What more sacred duty can man have than to cooperate in the destruction of this inequality—this want, on the one hand, and this temptation of riches on the other? And how can man cooperate in the destruction of these evils but by taking part in work which supplies human needs, and by liberating himself from superfluities and idleness productive of temptations and vices—how, that is, but by each man doing bread-labor to feed himself with his own hands, as Bondaref expresses it?

We have become so entangled, have involved ourselves in so many laws—religious, social, and family—have accepted so many precepts—as Isaiah says, precept upon precept, here a precept and there a precept—that we have completely lost the perception of what is good and what is bad.

One man performs Mass, another collects an army or the taxes to pay for it, a third acts as judge, a fourth studies books, a fifth heals people, a sixth instructs them, and freeing themselves from bread-labor under these pretexts, they thrust it on to others, and forget that men are dying of exhuastion, labor, and hunger; and that, in order that there may be people to sing Mass to, to defend with an army, to judge, to doctor, or to instruct, it is necessary, first of all, that they should not die of hunger. We forget that there may be many duties, but that among them all there is a first and a last, and that one must not fulfil the last before fulfilling the first, just as one must not harrow before plowing.

And it is to this first, undoubted duty in the sphere of practical activity, that Bondaref's teaching brings us back. Bondaref shows that the performance of this duty hinders nothing and presents no obstacles, yet saves men from the misery of want and temptation. Above all, the performance of this duty would destroy that terrible separation of mankind into two classes which hate each other and hide their mutual hatred by cajolery. Bread-labor, says Bondaref, equalizes all and clips the wings of luxury and lust.

One cannot plow or dig wells dressed in fine clothes, with clean hands, and nourishing one's self on delicate food. Work at one sacred occupation, common to all, will draw men together. Bread-labor, Bondaref says, will restore reason to those who have lost it by standing aside from the life natural to man, and will give happiness and content to those engaged in work undoubtedly useful, and appointed by God Himself and by the laws of Nature.

Bread-labor, says Bondaref, is a medicine to save mankind. If men acknowledged this first-born law as an unalterable law of God—if each one admitted bread-labor (to feed himself by the work of his own hands) to be his inexorable duty—all men would unite in belief in one God and in love one to another, and the sufferings which now weigh us down would be destroyed.

We are so accustomed to a way of life which assumes the opposite of this—namely, assumes that riches (means to avoid bread-labor) represent either a blessing from

God or a higher social status—that, without analyzing Bondaref's proposition, we wish to consider it narrow, one-sided, empty, and stupid. But we must examine his position carefully, and consider whether it be just or not.

We weigh all kinds of religious and political theories. Let us weigh Bondaref's also as a theory. Let us consider what the result will be if, in accord with his thought, the influence of religious teaching is directed to the elucidation of this commandment, and all men are brought to admit this sacred, first-born law of labor.

All will then work, and eat the fruit of their own labors. Corn and articles of primary necessity will cease to be objects of purchase or sale.

What will be the result?

The result will be that men will not perish from want. If from unfortunate circumstances one man fails to grow enough food for himself and his family, someone else, who from fortunate circumstances has grown too much, will supply the lack; and will do so the more readily because there is no other use for his corn, it being no longer an article of commerce. Then men will not be tempted by want to get their bread by cunning or by violence. And not being so tempted, they will not use cunning or violence; the need that now compels them will no longer exist.

If a man then still uses cunning or violence, it will be because he loves such ways, and not because they are necessary to him—as at present.

Nor will it be necessary for the weak—those who, for some reason, are unable to earn their bread, or who have lost it in any way—to sell themselves, their labor, or sometimes even their souls, for bread.

There will not be the present general striving to free one's self from bread-labor and to put it on to others—a

striving to crush the weak with overwork and to free the strong from all work.

There will not be that tendency which now directs the greatest efforts of man's minds, not towards lightening the labor of the workers, but towards lightening and embellishing the idleness of the idlers. The participation of all in bread-labor, and its recognition as first among human affairs, will accomplish what would be achieved by taking a cart, which stupid people were hauling along upside down, and turning it over on to its wheels. The cart would be saved from breaking, and would move easily.

And our life, with its contempt for, and rejection of, bread-labor, and our attempts at reforming that false life, are like a cart drawn along with its wheels in the air. All our reforms are useless till we turn the cart over and stand it right way up.

Such is Bondaref's thought with which I fully agree. The matter presents itself to me again as follows. There was a time when people ate one another. The consciousness of unity among men developed until that became impossible, and they ceased to eat each other. Then came a time when people seized the fruits of labor by violence from their fellows, and made slaves of men. But consciousness developed till that also became impossible. Violence, though still practiced in hidden ways, has been destroyed in its grosser forms: men no longer openly seize the fruits of another's labor.

In our day the form of violence practiced is, that some people take advantage of the needs of others to exploit them. In Bondaref's opinion the time is near when there will be such a perception of human unity that men will feel it impossible to take advantage of the need, the hunger, and the cold of others to exploit them; and when men, acknowledging the law of bread-labor as binding on everyone, will recognize it as their bounden duty, without selling articles of prime necessity, to feed, clothe, and warm one another in case of need.

Approaching the matter from another side, I look at this problem of Bondaref's thus: We often hear reflections on the insufficiency of merely negative laws or commandments—*i.e.*, of rules telling us what not to do. People say, We need positive laws or commandments—rules telling us what to do. The five commandments of Christ—(1) to consider no one insignificant or insane, and to be angry with no one; (2) not to consider sexual intercourse as a matter of pleasure, nor to leave the wife or husband with whom one has once united; (3) to take no oaths to anyone, and not to give away one's freedom; (4) to endure injuries and violence, and not to resist them by violence; and (5) to consider no man an enemy, but to love enemies as friends—it is said that these five commandments of Christ's all tell only what should not be done, but that there are no commandments or laws telling what should be done.

And, indeed, it may seem strange that in Christ's teaching there are no equally definite commandments telling us what we ought to do. But this seems strange only to those who do not believe Christ's real teaching, which is contained, not in five commandments, but in the teaching of truth itself.

The teaching of truth expressed by Christ is not contained in laws and commandments, but in one thing only—the meaning given to life. And that meaning is, that life and the blessing of life are not to be found in personal happiness, as people generally suppose, but in the service of God and man. And this is not a command which must be obeyed to gain a reward, nor is it a mystical expression of something mysterious and unintelligi-

The pastor sleeps. The noontime meal
Was ample, and the day is hot.
And Karo too is stuffed from head to heel.
A comfort now prevails of sated glut.

But while the pastor's sleeping for the nonce
A dream approaches—horrid and abhorred:
That he was truly, all at once,
As poor as Jesus Christ, Our Lord.

ble, but it is the elucidation of a law of life previously concealed; it is the indication of the fact that life can be a blessing only when this truth is understood.

And, therefore, the whole positive teaching of Christ is expressed in this one thing: Love God, and thy neighbor as thyself. And no expositions of that precept are possible. It is one, because it contains all.

The law and commandments of Christ, like the Jewish and Buddhist laws and commandments, are but indications of cases in which the snares of the world turn men aside from a true understanding of life. And that is why there may be many commandments, but the positive teaching of life—of what should be done—must and can be only one.

The life of each man is a movement somewhere: whether he will or not, he moves, he lives. Christ shows man the road, and at the same time indicates the paths leading from the right road—paths which lead astray. Of such indications there may be many—they are the commandments.

Christ gives five such commandments, and those he gave are such that up to the present not one can with advantage be added or spared. But only one direction showing the road is given, for there can be but one straight line showing a certain direction.

Therefore the idea that in Christ's teaching there are only negative commands and no positive ones seems true only to those who do not know, or do not believe, in the teaching of truth itself—the direction of the true path of life indicated by Christ. Believers in the truth of the path of life shown by Jesus will not seek for positive commandments in His teaching. All positive activity flowing from the teaching of the true path of life—most diverse as that activity may be—is always clearly and indubitably defined for them.

Believers in that path of life are, in Christ's simile, like an abundant spring of living water. All their activity is like the course of water, which flows everywhere regardless of obstacles. A man believing in the teaching of Christ can as little ask what positive commands he is to obey as a stream of water, bursting from the ground, could ask the question. It flows, watering the earth, grass, trees, birds, animals, and men. And a man who believes Christ's teaching of life does likewise.

A believer in the teaching of Jesus will not ask what he is to do. Love, which becomes the motive-force of his life, will surely and inevitably show him where to act, and what to do first and what afterwards.

Not to speak of indications Christ's teaching is full of, showing that the first and most necessary activity of love is to feed the hungry, give drink to the thirsty, clothe the naked, and help the poor and the prisoners,—our reason, conscience, and feelings all impel us (before undertaking any other service of love to living men) first to sustain life in our brethren by saving them from sufferings and death that threaten them in their too arduous struggles with Nature. That is to say, we are called on to share the labor needful for the life of man—the primary, rough, heavy labor on the land.

As a spring cannot question where its waters are to flow—upwards, splashing the grass and the leaves of the trees, or downwards to the roots of the grass and trees—so a believer in the teaching of truth cannot ask what he must do first—whether to teach people, defend them, amuse them, supply them with the pleasures of life, or save them from perishing of want. And just as water from a spring flows along the surface and fills ponds and gives drink to animals and men, only after it has soaked the ground, so a believer in the teaching of truth can serve less urgent human demands only after he has satisfied the primary demand: has helped to feed men, and to save them from perishing in their struggle against want.

A man following the teaching of truth and love, not in words but in deeds, cannot mistake where first to direct his efforts. A man who sees the meaning of his life in service to others can never make such a blunder as to begin to serve hungry and naked humanity by forging cannon, manufacturing elegant ornaments, or playing the violin or the piano.

Love cannot be stupid.

As love for one man would not let us read novels to him who was starving, or hang costly earrings on him who was naked, so love for mankind will not let us serve it by amusing the well-fed while we leave the cold and hungry to die of want.

True love, love not merely in words but in deeds, cannot be stupid—it is the one thing giving true perception and wisdom.

And, therefore, a man penetrated by love will not make a mistake, but will be sure to do first what love of man first requires: he will do what maintains the life of the hungry, the cold, and the heavy-laden, and *that* is all done by a direct struggle with Nature.

Only he who wishes to deceive himself and others, can, while men are in danger, struggling against want, stand aside from helping them, and while he adds to their burden, assure himself and those who perish before his eyes, that he is occupied, or is devising means to save them.

No sincere man who sees that the purpose of his life is to serve others will say that. Or if he says it, he will find in his conscience no confirmation of his delusion, but will have to seek it in the insidious doctrine of the division of labor. In all expressions of true human wisdom, from Confucius to Muhammad, he will find one and the same truth (and will find it most forcibly in the Gospels)—a summons to serve man not according to the theory of the division of labor, but in the simplest, most natural, and only necessary way: he will find a demand to serve the sick, the prisoners, the hungry, and the naked. And help to the sick, the prisoners, the hungry, and the naked, can be rendered only by one's own immediate direct labor—for the sick, hungry, and naked do not wait, but die of hunger and cold.

His own life, which consists of service to others, will guide a man confessing the teaching of truth, to that primary law expressed at the commencement of Genesis, "In the sweat of thy face shalt thou eat bread," which Bondaref calls "first-born" and puts forward as a positive command.

And positive that law really is, for those who do not acknowledge the meaning of life which Christ disclosed. Such it was for men before Christ, and such it remains for those who do not acknowledge Christ's teaching. It demands that everyone should—according to the law of God expressed in the Bible and in our reason—feed himself by his own labor. That law was positive, and such it remains till the meaning of life is revealed to man by the teaching of truth.

But from the plane of the higher consciousness of life disclosed by Christ, the law of bread-labor, remaining true as before, fits into Christ's one positive teaching of service to man; and must be regarded no longer as positive, but as negative. That law, from the Christian point of view, merely indicates an ancient snare, and tells

men what they should avoid in order not to stray from the path of true life.

For a follower of the Old Testament who does not acknowledge this teaching of truth, this law means: "Produce thy bread by the labor of thine own hands." But for a Christian its meaning is negative. To him this law says: "Do not suppose it possible to serve men while you consume what others labor to produce and do not produce your own maintenance with your own hands."

This law, for a Christian, is an indication of one of the most ancient and terrible of the temptations from which mankind suffers. Against that temptation (terrible in its consequences, and so old that it is hard for us to admit that it is not a natural characteristic of man, but a deception) this teaching of Bondaref is directed—a teaching equally obligatory on a believer in the Old Testament, on a Christian who believes in the Gospels, and on him who disbelieves in the Bible and follows only common-sense.

There is much I could and would write to prove the truth of this position and overthrow the various and complex arguments against it which rise to the lips of us all; we know we are to blame, and are therefore always ready with justifications. But however much I may write, however well I may write, and however logically exact I may be, I shall not convince my reader, so long as his intellect is pitted against mine and his heart remains cold.

And that is why I ask you, reader, to check for awhile the activity of your intellect, and not to argue nor to demonstrate, but to ask only your heart. Whoever you may be, however gifted, however kind to those about you, however circumstanced, can you sit unmoved over your tea, your dinner, your political, artistic, scientific, medical, or educational affairs, while you hear or see at your door a hungry, cold, sick, suffering man? No. Yet they are always there, if not at the door, then ten yards or ten miles away. They are there, and you know it.

And you cannot be at peace—cannot have pleasure which is not poisoned by this knowledge. Not to see them at your door you have to fence them off, or keep them away by your coldness, or go somewhere where they are not. But they are everywhere.

And if a place be found where you cannot see them, still, you can nowhere escape from the truth. What, then, must be done?

You know these things, and the teaching of truth tells you them.

Go to the bottom—to what seems to you the bottom, but is really the top—take your place beside those who produce food for the hungry and clothes for the naked, and do not be afraid: it will not be worse, but better in all respects. Take your place in the ranks, set to work with your weak, unskilled hands at that primary work which feeds the hungry and clothes the naked: at bread-labor, the struggle with Nature; and you will feel, for the first time, firm ground beneath your feet, will feel that you are at home, that you are free and stand firmly, and have reached the end of your journey. And you will feel those complete, unpoisoned joys which can be found nowhere else—not secured by any doors nor screened by any curtains.

You will know joys you have never known before; you will, for the first time, know those strong, plain men, your brothers, who from a distance have fed you until now; and to your surprise you will find in them such qualities as you have never known: such modesty, such kindness to yourself as you will feel you have not deserved.

Instead of the contempt or scorn you expected, you will meet with such kindness, such gratitude and respect for having—after living on them and despising them all your life—at last recollected yourself, and with unskilled hands tried to help them.

You will see that what seemed to you like an island on which you were saved from the sea that threatened to engulf you, was a marsh in which you were sinking; and the sea you feared was dry land on which you will walk firmly, quietly, and happily; as must be the case, for from a deception (into which you did not enter of your own wish, but into which you were led) you will escape to the truth, and from the evasion of God's purpose you will pass to its performance.

24

The Magazine of Living the Way
—Twenty-four Hours at a Time

The following is a brief description of *24 Magazine*. For information about subscription ($10 for 12 issues) and back issues ($1 each), address all communications to *24 Magazine*, Hankins, N.Y. 12741.

If you have no interest in the Way—or if you are an exclusive partisan of some aspect of the Way—you will find *24 Magazine* pointless or an actual pain in the neck. On the other hand, if you do have a live interest in the Way and are not in a sectarian lock-in, you may find *24 Magazine* interesting and helpful.

What is the Way? We have taken the trouble to make as clear and concise a statement of it as we are able, and we run this on an early page in each issue of the magazine—as follows:

> The Way is a method, a program, a means, and a power for achieving a definite result: a radical change (metanoia) in human consciousness and human nature, bringing with it freedom from want and fear, regeneration of the whole person, and the true brotherhood of man. It is no small thing, but small and weak people can do it, indeed are peculiarly qualified to do it. The Way is not a religion, but all real reli-

gion springs from it—not a science, but all real science obeys its principles—not an art, but all real art is a communication of it. The Way is the power which keeps the stars in their courses, and shows men how to live. It is the way the universe works, and it is the way *you* work when you are in your right mind. It is the Norm of human life. People are sane when they obey it, and insane when they ignore it. The Way is what the rationalists call the First Principles of Practical Reason and the faithful call the Kingdom of Heaven. All things are made by it, supported by it, and received by it at death. The Way is the Life (Zoe). It is the Law (Torah) and the Presence (Shekinah), the Road (Tariqa) and the Struggle (Akbar), the Path (Tao) and its Power (Teh), the Pattern (Rita) and the Method (Dharma). It is Logos-Sophia, Atman, the ruling Power of the universe in its aspect of illuminator and guide of the human race. It is the Truth, the ultimate Reality, the Self-existent, the Suchness—Altheia, Sat, al-Haqq, Aehyeh, Tathata. It is Christ, God himself as teacher, helper, friend, and savior of men. It is the King of kings and Lord of lords, the blessed and only Potentate. It is all this at one and the same time. And whether you like it or not, or believe it or not, you are dealing with it—positively or negatively—every hour of your life. To read about the Way, or just to think about it, is not enough. You need a definite program of action, and you need to be in touch with others who are working the same program. In this century, a real Program for living the Way, twenty-four hours at a time, has appeared in the Twelve Steps of Alcoholics Anonymous. This program works not only for alcoholics but, with very simple adaptations, for anyone.

The Way is the most conspicuous item in the entire human landscape—and yet it is now very hard to find. The most striking peculiarity of modern times is the fact that the Way—this single, central, overwhelming concern of mankind over all the ages—is now obscured in a manner never before known on earth. The rejection of the Way—the subversion, ridicule, and widespread studied ignorance of the Way, notably among the intellectual leaders of the race and subsequently inevitably among people of every kind and condition—all this in the last third of the 20th Century has reached the point of near-total eclipse of the Way. The most important thing that every man, woman, and child needs to know is taught almost nowhere, honored almost nowhere, *available* almost nowhere—unless you are ready to make a very special effort.

Even so, the monuments of the Way—the literature, the art, the music, and the architecture of the Way—are to be found everywhere, still. And the people of the Way are scattered throughout the population, still. The Way is a possible resource for anyone who will seek it, and the only resource for people in certain kinds of trouble. The Way continues to be what is has always been—the *only way out* of the deep sicknesses of man—the one power which provides full deliverance from the real spiritual sloughs of humanity: the compulsions, the addictions, the fears, the depressions, the outright insanities, and the fog of meaninglessness which now creeps in on people everywhere.

STRENGTH BOOKS

A Division of East Ridge Press

God is our refuge and strength. Around this truth, STRENGTH Books are edited. These are books about God, and the Way to God. Books about religion properly so-called: rebinding to God, yoga, union with Reality. Books about higher consciousness, training for the life of the spirit, triumphant life in God. Books about the inspired men and women of God, the great exemplars of the Way, the bridge builders and pathfinders for the human race—the fathers and mothers—the avataras, buddhas, and boddhisattvas—the seers, priests, patriarchs, prophets, apostles, confessors, and martyrs—the saints, ascetics and hermits—the friends of God and servants of God in all ages and all places. Books about the literature, art, doctrine, and tradition of the Way to God, both exoteric and esoteric. Books about the triple paths of generation, degeneration and regeneration. Books about Messias, his coming and his kingdom; the beginning, middle, and end of the world; the fall, struggle, and salvation of man. Books of all peoples, of all times, and of the timeless. Books designed to help us to claim the primordial promise: to find our way to God, our refuge, our strength, our certainty, our fulfillment, and our deliverance from all ill.

$7.50

THE WAY TO **HIGHER CONSCIOUSNESS**

Edited by Meredith Murray and the Editors of 24 Magazine

A STRENGTH BOOK

The great secret of human life is to discover the singular Person who dwells serenely in the midst of the plural babble of our personality. Our name is Legion. His name is One.

(See listing, page 161)

The secret and the mystery of higher consciousness—the state characterized by total absence of fear and uncertainty and by awareness of overwhelming love and beauty—is inseparable from the mystery of the Self. The Self is a matter of intimate and inescapable everyday experience, and yet the experience is profoundly distorted and continuously misunderstood. With the result that, as a matter of practical fact, the man does not know himself.

This is the most conspicuous feature of our present humanity. It is the core of the human problem and the key to its solution, and every authentic school of regeneration begins at this point. All of the great religions offer to man a way of return to knowledge of, and re-union with, the Self.

The Way to Higher Consciousness defines the actual experience of this kind of consciousness in telling the stories—in their own words—of some of the greatest men of all time: Muhammad, St. Paul, Moses, Plato—and the more contemporary stories of Frank Buchman (founder of The Oxford Groups), Bill Wilson (co-founder of Alcoholics Anonymous), and Richard M. Bucke (author of *Cosmic Consciousness*).

But *The Way to Higher Consciousness* is more than a description of that state—it is a practical workbook designed to help readers to move toward actual attainment of it. The state of Self-awareness, higher consciousness, is each man's birthright. This book is about regaining access to that glorious endowment which we men lost eons ago when we departed from our primal estate and our Author.

(See listing, page 161)

Sacred Sex

Edited by Thomas R. White and the Editors of 24 Magazine

A STRENGTH BOOK

Sacred Sex is a unique summary of the esoteric truths of true *Tantra,* which is no mere oriental curiosity or hippie turn-on but *the* way to God for married people, Western or Eastern, in this modern age—the elevation of sex to the sacred, God-centered, blissful function it was ordained to be.

This book is about three different kinds of sex: (1) *Sick Sex* —a wide range of sick practices, in fantasy and actuality, including adultery, fornication, masturbation, homosexuality, exhibitionism, and other perversions. (2) *Sane Sex*—married sex, kept well within the framework of the marriage vows. (3) *Sacred Sex*—for both married and unmarried people, the offering to God of the greatest sensate joy and treasure we can give, and receiving in return God's gift to us of supreme love and bliss.

Sex is divine creative power. God, who is incredibly permissive even in the matter of his highest gifts, gives us freedom to use it as we will. But the Way—the Universal Spiritual Tradition of all mankind—has always said that we cannot escape the creative factor in sex. Neither can we escape the gift of responsibility which goes with the gift of freedom. The Way says finally that there is a mystery in sex, a question of the Sphinx, which when answered leads to the fulfillment of man's highest possibilities.

Sacred Sex is, first, an incisive disclosure by four editors of *24 Magazine* of their own years of trouble with sex—of trying to have sex without responsibility, of trying to make sick sex work, of trying to justify excesses and perversions. And then it is the record of their *turning,* of their conversion to a radical new approach to sex which, as it happens, is also the immemorial sexual standard of the human race, a standard based on the understanding that of all the sacred things in life, sex is one of the very most sacred.

160

STRENGTH BOOKS

MODERN SPIRITUAL PRACTICE

Sacred Sex. *Thomas R. White, ed.* A unique summary of the esoteric truths of true *Tantra*, which is no mere oriental curiosity but *the* way to God for married men and women, Western or Eastern, in this age. 120 pp. 4¼x7 Profusely illus.
LC 74-84538   ISBN 0-914896-01-6   **$1.95**

Breakthrough to God: The Ultimate Experiment. By *Thomas E. Powers.* How a tough materialist went through crisis to experience of the one great Truth: God exists, *and we can know him.* A handbook for other experimenters.   336 pp. 5¼ x 8¼ Biblio. May 1975.
LC 74-16887   ISBN 0-914896-02-4   **$4.95**

Training for the Life of the Spirit. *Gerald Heard.* One of the most incisive of modern minds shows that prayer and meditation are the only means to further human evolution, and shows the way to pursue it. 144 pp. 4¼ x 7 Illus. May 1975
LC 74-29127   ISBN 0-914896-11-3   **$2.50**

SELF KNOWLEDGE

The Way to Higher Consciousness. *Meredith Murray, ed.* A map of the levels of consciousness, from sleep to illumination. A practical guide to the place in ourselves which is our blessed homeland. 136 pp. 4¼ x 7 Profusely illus.

LC 74-16879   ISBN 0-914896-09-1   **$2.50**

DRUGS AND THE SPIRITUAL LIFE

Why Do Men Stupefy Themselves? *Leo Tolstoy.* Surgical probing by the great Russian of three prime trouble spots in modern life: drugs, fake Christianity, and middle class idleness and self-indulgence. 168 pp. 4¼ x 7 Profusely illus. March 1975.

LC 74-16880   ISBN 0-914896-08-3   **$2.50**

SPIRITUAL CLASSICS

The God-Illuminated Cook: The Practice of the Presence of God. *Brother Lawrence.* A beautiful new edition, with special commentary revealing the hidden depths beneath the simplicities of the great spiritual classic. 144 pp. 4¼ x 7 Profusely illus. March 1975.

LC 74-83499   ISBN 0-914896-00-8   **$2.50**

THE SUPERNATURAL

Death and Then What? *Thomas E. Powers and Christopher Stein.* A primer—based on massive evidence from the sources of authentic reporting and real knowledge—of death and the after-death experience of mankind. 120 pp. 4¼ x 7 Profusely illus. Biblio. June 1975.

LC 74-16886   ISBN 0-914896-03-2   **$1.95**

MODERN CHRISTIAN KNOWLEDGE

Nothing Burns in Hell but the Ego. *Robin Dawes, ed.* A new presentation of Susannah Winkworth's translation

The
God-Illuminated
Cook

A new edition of *The Practice of the Presence of God* by
Brother Lawrence

A new presentation of a great spiritual classic,
illustrated with mandalas from the Book of Kells,
and edited by the Editors of 24 Magazine

A STRENGTH BOOK

(See listing, page 162)

This book—one of the great spiritual treasures of all time—is the legacy of an extraordinary man who spent his entire adult life working in a kitchen. It is well known to be among the great helping resources of the theocentric life. What is not so well known is the fact that this celebrated small treatise on the path to God is easily misunderstood. Although it is highly esteemed, it is in fact widely underestimated. Its beautiful simplicity overlays, and for a casual reader is apt to conceal, its immense range and depth of meaning.

The new Strength edition deals with the difficulties as well as the simplicities, and it offers an unusual combination of contemporaneity, convenience, readability, utility, and beauty. While acknowledging and honoring the historic and traditional stature of *The Practice of the Presence*, this edition views it preeminently as a spiritual guide and workbook peculiarly well adapted to the problem of cleaving to God in the modern world. The introduction presents the book in a new way; it is concerned incidentally with the details of the book's origins and the life of its author, but mainly and centrally it deals with *The Practice of the Presence* as a practical spiritual tool of special relevance and usefulness for men and women of today, and it discusses in detail the strange, baffling, and exhilarating problems of actually applying Brother Lawrence's method in daily life now.

163

(See listing, page 161)

BREAKTHROUGH TO GOD

By Thomas E. Powers
and the Editors of 24 Magazine

A STRENGTH BOOK

$4.95

THE ULTIMATE EXPERIMENT

When this extraordinary testament and work manual first appeared (under the title *First Questions on the Life of the Spirit*), Louis Cassels of United Press International wrote of it: "For those who are already tentatively or securely committed to a religious faith, this book offers a guide toward a deeper understanding of the spiritual life. For those who do not believe in God, but who are troubled by what G.K. Chesterton called 'the first wild doubts of doubt,' it is a compelling invitation to a great experiment."

In the preface to this new edition, Powers writes: " 'Experiment' is the keynote of our entire cultural epoch. We have not been content to take anything on hearsay or traditional authority but have wanted to try everything out for ourselves. We have experimented with everything within range of the human mind. With one exception. We have made no experiment upon God. The omission is striking. We have scientifically tested every imaginable datum, except the most elementary, most obvious, and most inescapable datum of all. Why? I think we do not seek God experimentally, scientifically, without fear or favor *because we are afraid of what the result might be*. It might turn out that God is real after all—and the discovery of him would unhinge our world."

Breakthrough to God has played a remarkable part in the growth of groups of spiritual seekers throughout the country who have used it as a basis for their study and experimental work. It is a clear, concise, step-by-step workbook for men and women who are awake both to the futilities and to the unusual opportunities of our times and who are looking for a practical path to spiritual regeneration.

of the *Theologia Germanica*, the classic manual that tells how to reduce egotism and how finally to get rid of it. 208 pp. 4¼x7 June 1975.

LC 74-16882 ISBN 0-914896-06-7   **$2.50**

Your bookseller has these titles or can get them for you. For mail orders, please add 30¢ per book to cover postage and handling. Prices subject to change without notice.

Strength Books are not only written and/or edited but also designed, set in type, and printed by the same community of Wayfarers who produce *24 Magazine*. This volume is set in 10 point English No. 49 type on the Compuwriter, and printed on 60-pound Hamilton Vellum Opaque paper, on a Solna 164 offset press.